The Ultimate Networking Machine

Become Willing, Become Wealthy

By Kale Goodman

Foreword by Ryan Stewman

The Ultimate Networking Machine: Become Willing, Become Wealthy

All Rights Reserved

COPYRIGHT © 2022 Kale Goodman

This book may not be reproduced, transmitted, or stored in whole or in part by any means, including graphic, electronic, or mechanical, without the express written consent of the publisher except in the case of brief questions embodied in critical articles and reviews.

ISBN: 979-8-9856052-0-4

Cover design by Sooraj Matthew

Edited by Hilary Jastram, Bookmark Publishing House, JHilCreative.com

DEDICATION

To my wife Kaylee for her immense support, you see my greatness and potential, sometimes more so than I see in myself. It's so encouraging to have you by my side, and your love fuels me to continue to be my best self. I love you.

To my current and past business partners for all our great learning experiences and the journeys we have been on.

To my parents and siblings, I appreciate all the experiences and lessons you've shared with me—lessons that have furthered my growth and that will now help the readers of this book. I've overcome, learned, and grown so much from our crazy bunch. We have experienced love and pain, comfort and chaos, tough times, and happy times. Thank you for what you have taught me.

RESOURCES

To get in touch with Kale and learn more about becoming an Ultimate Marketing Machine, visit KaleGoodman.com.

TABLE OF CONTENTS

Foreword 1

Introduction 1

Chapter 1 – Are You a Part of Your Strategy? 1

Chapter 2 – Rewiring Your Thinking to Become an Ultimate Networker 1

Chapter 3 – Sales is a Foundation 1

Chapter 4 – The Closer Culture 1

Chapter 5 – More Money, More Opportunity 1

Chapter 6 – Taking the Leap 1

Chapter 7 – The Magic Formula of Wealth and Networking 1

Chapter 8 – The Hard Cuts That Need To Happen 1

Chapter 9 – Step in a New Direction 1

Chapter 10 – Pre-Judgment is a Cost! 1

Chapter 11 – Greed Kills 1

Chapter 12 – How to Avoid Being Greedy in Business 1

Chapter 13 – Building and Evaluating Your Business 1

Chapter 14 – Elevating Your Business 1

Chapter 15 – Magnetic Moves 1

Chapter 16 – Strong Leadership Creates Your Bulletproof Reputation 1

Acknowledgments 1

About The Author 1

FOREWORD

In every story we've ever been told about any industry or entity, there's always been a disruption.

After a certain way of operating for a long period of time, for some reason or another, a disruption came.

When that happened, it changed everything.

People used to communicate face to face, for example. Then the telephone was invented. This disruption altered the course of mankind.

Industries have been interrupted by titans like Steve Jobs and Bill Gates. They have been created by visionaries like Sergey Brin, Larry Page, Mark Zuckerberg, and Jack Dorsey, who have interrupted the interrupters.

Yet some businesses that have been around since practically the dawn of time have never experienced a disruption. Those industries include real estate, banking, financial advising, tax collecting, and accounting.

Accounting is as old as the Bible. Ironically, the Bible talks about Jesus hanging out with tax collectors and accountants. Today, nobody on the entire planet likes accounting or taxes, but the people who benefit from them—the tax collectors and accountants.

Despite the rest of the world despising everything about this system, this industry has never had any disruptions. It is what it always is: a bunch of boring motherfuckers telling you that you owe money to a bunch of scamming motherfuckers who label themselves the government.

I said it.

That's the way we're kicking off this book.

Now, the disruption is happening in the accounting industry right before our eyes and within the pages of this book.

That's because my friend, Kale Greatman—I call him that even though his last name is Goodman because he's a great man, not just a good man—is changing the way that age-old, stale industry works. For the first time in history, he's making accounting sexy, fun, and less painful.

So, how did a person like Kale take an ancient system and disrupt, so that the people around him actually care about taxes, financial advice, and the less glamourous tasks they loathe doing?

The story of how Kale was able to do that is what lies between the rest of the pages of this book.

Now, you have an opportunity to learn from somebody who is in real-time a disruptor in an industry. This is rare because we typically don't hear about disruptors until they've passed or after quite a few years have gone by.

Ten to 15 years after Mark Zuckerberg started what would become the Meta, we finally heard about how he'd disrupted the industry. Of course, people tried to prevent him from starting a new industry. They didn't want him to be a disruption. The media doesn't talk about disruptions unless it fits their agenda. So by the time we hear about disruptors, they've already rocked the status quo.

I don't know what year in the future you're reading this book. But if it's around the time I wrote this foreword in 2022, the accounting disruption is happening now. Not only will you be on the cutting edge of this massive change, but you will also get the background story, the blueprint, and the pages that follow Kale accordingly.

FOREWORD

In my history of running businesses, writing books, and coaching, I've never had the chance to see and read a plan of disruption while it was taking place.

Until now.

Since you're reading this book, we get to both share that privilege.

Keep turning the pages and find out just what Kale did to wake up an industry and change the way it does business forever.

Rise Above,
Ryan Stewman

INTRODUCTION

As I write this book, I'm crossing over into fifteen years in business as an entrepreneur.

Building multiple businesses has taught me so much in that time. That's why I'm writing a book—to share everything I have learned with you.

My hopes n writing this book are that my lessons can help many other entrepreneurs achieve in their first five years what I have achieved in my last five years in business. And these most recent years have been the most rewarding. I have seen the most growth both in business and my personal life during this time.

I credit that to the focus I put on networking. It has been the catapult to create what has been built and the success I've experienced in my businesses.

To move the needle as much as possible toward my goals, I used specific systems and key components to network to the best of my abilities. In the coming pages, I am breaking them all down for you. Keep reading, and you will learn from the stories I share and the lessons I had to discover of what worked and what didn't.

I'll share some key fundamentals in business that will help you become an Ultimate Networking Machine in your business. You can apply fundamentals like how to use your money as a proper tool to network, how to build your team around you, how to strategically align yourself with your ideal customers, referral partners, vendors, and employees, and how to build great friendships within those relationships.

Business is a game of relationships which is why it's so important to make networking one of your major priorities.

We must be strategic and tactical in how we build our network. One of the greatest strategies in networking involves not only aligning yourself with ideal people but learning how to become an attractive person in business. You want to bring the ideal people to you!

The only way to do that is to transform into a person of willingness. That means you are willing to own your shit and work on and become a greater version of yourself. Aim for becoming a person others seek to be around and do business with.

I start this book by explaining the miles I have come, so you will believe in yourself. So you will see my past as history that ties us. Every person has hardships. I was no different. I was a messed up angry soul who pushed all the people around me away. As a high school dropout and teenage parent at barely eighteen years old, I was a master at participating in toxic relationships. Through the years and until I discovered what I was capable of, I was constantly starting over because I didn't have the confidence to finish anything.

I can't even relate to that version of me anymore. I am now a person of willingness. I have the willingness to embark on a journey of personal growth and become honest about who I was, as I recognized how to do the work to transform into who I am now.

Now, I am a person who feels so much more happiness, who knows much more success. People want to win with me in life and be around me. I am grateful for that every day.

The biggest takeaway I hope you will consider is that the lessons I share are the gateway to a better life. I decided to make becoming a better me the strategy to win at business and life. It has been the absolute best action I could take to give me the personal and business results I want. It will be for you as well.

Enjoy the read, and make sure you implement what you learn here so you can enjoy the ride, too.

Chapter 1

ARE YOU A PART OF YOUR STRATEGY?

"When everything seems to be against you, remember that the airplane takes off against the wind, not with it."
—Henry Ford

I was in a therapist's office because I was sick of me. For so long, I had tried to break out of a rut in my relationships and life. My marriage had just ended. I was a furious man, and every time I tried to make a change for the better, it didn't work.

After marriage counseling failed, my therapist Steve gave me a harsh truth—that I had needed to hear for a long time.

He locked eyes with me and said, "Kale, I'd love to help you become a person of quality and happiness, but I don't think you're ready for that. It will take a lot of work, and most people aren't up for it."

If you know me, you know what my response was.

"I am willing to do the work," I told him.

I'll never forget what he said next.

Steve stared me dead in the eyes and stated, "Our thoughts create our emotions. Our emotions influence our actions. And our actions create who we are."

This was the healing journey I had wanted for so long!

Steve explained, "We have to begin by practicing new thoughts. There are many ways we can get started doing that, but research shows that it takes three to five years to rewire our thoughts so that we think in this new way naturally. Right now, you're hard-wired to think the way you do."

I nodded along as he spoke. I just knew this conversation was different. My life was about to change.

"We have to reverse your thoughts," Steve said, "Think about it like this. You have had patterns of thoughts for years that have directly influenced the way you naturally think now. So, trying to think differently in the short term is not going to work. We have to create exercises that you will need to do over and over for the next three to five years until you gravitate almost instinctively to your new hard-wired thinking. Just like your muscles need consistent exercise to grow, develop and reshape, your brain works in the same way. It needs regular workouts to grow, develop and reshape it as well."

After that conversation, Steve and I completed a few sessions, and then I had my moment of reckoning.

It hurt.

But understanding where my self-judgment came from and healing it was the only way out of the cyclical hell I had created myself.

I had to face what had been haunting me my whole life, what had told me I wasn't worth much.

"What's wrong with me, Steve?" I asked one day, sounding like a little kid. "Why am I not enough?" As I slouched there in my chair facing him and his gentle smile, the truth swam into focus.

"Let's dig a little more to find the answer to your question."

I swallowed since I didn't trust myself to speak yet. All I could do was stare at Steve with tears in my eyes.

Before I go any further, I need to clarify that my parents are amazing people who taught me great things. I know their intention was never to create specific messaging or wire a mindset of limited thinking for their children. I know they acted out of love and fear and felt they were raising their kids the best they could. We all try to raise our children better than we were raised. My parents definitely accomplished that. They gave me so much more than they had in their upbringings. I am just grateful that I faced the challenges I did because they gave me the power to choose a new way of thinking, a new identity, and a new personality. I am not a victim of my parents. I know I would not have had the growth I've experienced without them. I only share a part of my journey with you to empower you to know that you do have a choice to rewire yourself. You can design yourself to be ultimate in whatever you choose. I love my parents deeply and am so glad they are such a present part of my life again. I give thanks for their tough love when I needed it.

But back then, I was still in therapy with Steve and had shared horrible stories of emotional and mental abuse from my mother. At one appointment, Steve pressed gently, "What about your dad? What kind of messaging did you get from him?"

As I write this, I know how weird it sounds. My mom and dad were complete opposites.

"I don't know, Steve. My dad was great in a lot of ways, but he was absent for many things, too. He worked a ton of hours and worked hard. But he also did cool things, like help coach our football games. My dad's messaging was quite the opposite of my mother's. He'd say things like, 'You're the fastest kid in town' or 'You can beat any of those guys.' He tried hard to instill in his children that we were better than the other kids, that we were capable. He encouraged us to be strong."

A new thought was stirring behind Steve's eyes. I could tell by his expression. He said, "It's radical that you developed a lot of your internal beliefs off your mom's messaging instead of your dad's messaging."

That one stumped me, too. You would think I would run toward the person who hurt me less. But then we got a little bit deeper and figured out why there was such a difference as to who I listened to and why.

My dad's messaging centered around telling us kids that we were capable of being whatever we wanted to be.

That would've been great to hear if his life had shown us that he was living his words.

But his life was contradictory to the messages he tried to get us to believe.

What Steve and I discovered through therapy and the practice of looking for patterns is that it was hard to adapt my dad's messaging when he wasn't living what he was speaking. I could see his financial struggles and relationship problems. He couldn't hide the problems that surrounded him. That took away some of his credibility. He was constantly in a tough situation and wasn't elevating himself. So it was nearly impossible to adapt his messaging of being a confident person when he wasn't living what he needed to do to become that way.

On the flip side, it was easier to adapt my mom's messaging that there was something wrong with me. But doing that led to me questioning everything I thought. When I got into trouble, I would remember what she said, believe I was stupid, and that I made stupid decisions.

This new thought process was dangerous to a degree. It seemed like a free pass to act horribly and get away with it.

But I refused to stay in this hurtful mindset. I wanted more for myself.

Learning to Believe in Myself

After more sessions with Steve, I discovered what was holding me back and how to heal it so I could move past it for good.

Becoming an Ultimate Networking Machine has everything to do with believing in yourself. I never could've moved forward without addressing what was wrong in my life and the low self-worth I had.

That's why I bring this all up. Going to therapy was the turning point for me. I didn't want the life I had created anymore. I wanted a different one I could get excited about.

If you are relating to this, whether you go to therapy, work with a coach, or find something else that works for you, please follow through. Work on yourself.

Rewiring yourself will also attract the right people to you—this is the networking secret that I want to share with you. It's a secret not many people know about.

It might not seem groundbreaking, but I am telling you, my whole life is different. The people who are attracted to me are different. Now, I have people at much higher levels who want to do business with me because of the work I have done on myself. After you get yourself straightened out, it's inevitable that you will work with the people you are supposed to—so you can be the greatest version of yourself.

Since I was Young

When I was a kid, all I ever wanted to be was a businessman and investor. I imagined launching amazing companies and making investments that would pay off.

It took willingness to turn that dream into a reality—to design my life to match my dream.

> **Becoming a person of willingness will also help you create the life you want—by your design.**

Designing my life required two factors:

1. The willingness to change.

2. A network of amazing people.

As I told you, I didn't figure this out right away, and I didn't always have a strong will and solid network. It took work to build them. In my case, it's more accurate to say that I had to rebuild them.

I'd always been the person who had to start over, so I should have been good at this rebuilding thing. Living in chaos and needing to redo what I tried also made me a real joy to be around. I tended to sabotage any good strides I'd taken. It took me years to learn how to leave the rough cycle behind.

Over the last decade, I've considered myself a person possessing a higher level of awareness. Instead of mindlessly watching my life burn, I now know when I am sabotaging myself.

Take These Lessons

Now that you have a better understanding of where I started, I want you to apply my breakthrough to your life. Think about how many areas of my existence have changed. Then consider if you walk through the same mental challenges, you will learn things about yourself that you thought were long-buried.

What I discovered about myself has not only helped me in my networking, in my business, but it has benefitted the people on my teams and assisted them in becoming more capable.

In the next chapter, I'll teach you a couple of exercises that my therapist taught me that changed the game for me. Do these exercises and apply them to your life, and they will change the game for you, too.

Before I could begin therapy, I had to find the willingness to consider it. Then I had to make the commitment to myself to actually hire someone. I continued to be willing as Steve and I worked together despite the stigma people might have thought about me—of being weak or not mentally sound. I was and am willing to go down rocky roads and don't care what people think. Today, I am so glad I went to therapy. The exercises I learned and applied to my life have been incredibly impactful to my trajectory.

Regardless of the stigma, please be willing to do the work. It can help you.

It is my hope that after you go through the exercises in the next chapter that you will be able to pass them on to other people and help them, too.

Chapter 2

Rewiring Your Thinking To Become An Ultimate Networker

"By becoming self-aware, you gain ownership of reality; in becoming real, you become the master of both inner and outer life."
—Deepak Chopra

I can't stress enough how much allowing my personal upbringing and programming to fester limited my beliefs and confidence in myself and held me back from connecting with people and creating positive relationships. I was an angry person who lashed out at the world, and that got me nothing but more anger, frustration, and fewer opportunities to be happy.

In healing what was holding me back, I realized that relationships are our most valuable commodity—not only in our personal lives but in our business lives as well.

When it came to working with Steve, we had to create a new way of thinking for me. This rewired programming would give me the life I wanted. I'll be honest with you. At the time I committed to these exercises, my intent was not to increase my business relationships. I was hurt emotionally. My only goal was to feel happiness and become a better example for my children.

Steve explained that one thought alone doesn't form your self-image. It takes an accumulation of those thoughts or experiences to build the way we feel about ourselves.

> **The key to our freedom of thought is to control what we think about, so we can shape our own perception of reality.**

I wanted freedom from my anger and so badly to be different. But more than anything, I wanted to be happy!

Thank goodness for me, Steve was not just skilled in reprogramming; he had useful and life-altering exercises up his sleeve.

A.B.C.D.E.

An exercise developed by a Dr. Ellis is called A.B.C.D.E. Steve advised me to try it during one of our sessions and printed out a worksheet that walks you through a new thought process each time you feel triggered by an unwanted thought or emotion.

It's pretty complex, but I've broken it down for you here:

A = Activating Event. These are the events in your life that caused you to lose your shit. In this A phase, you must become honest with yourself about how you feel about the event and why it happened in the first place.

Each day I would go home and fill out however many sheets I could depending on the number of activating events that had occurred.

For example, kicking a chair at my employee for talking back to me in a way I perceived as disrespectful, flipping someone off in traffic for cutting me off, or screaming at my ex-wife in front of my kids. These are great examples of things I would do.

B = Belief. In this step, you dig a little bit deeper than you did when you were trying to dredge up the activating event. The goal is to find the *belief of the event* that you allowed to cause your reaction.

Because our subconscious runs us so much, we don't take the time to try and understand what we believe our underlying fears are before we react.

REWIRING YOUR THINKING
TO BECOME AN ULTIMATE NETWORKER

Let's use the example of me screaming at my ex-wife in front of my children. As I am filling out my sheet, I would question what my true belief was that allowed my unwanted behavior.

When you find the belief, you will feel it. An honest assessment will arise, so you can see the truth. In this situation, I could've been scared that my children were bonding more with her than me on our rotating weeks. So, I yelled at her and called her names in front of the kids, hoping they would side with me or think less of her. (I know it's horrible, but we can't make changes without being honest.) After I wrote down my true and honest fear, I moved on to C.

C = Consequence. When I reached this stage, I would write down the consequence of the activating event and fear that I had authorized. In my scenario, the consequence was the damage it did to my children when I attempted to create a wedge between my boys and their mother. I was able to delve even deeper than the circumstances driving my fear. I acknowledged that it was possible my behavior had something to do with the long-held resentment of *my* mother. Recreating any sort of similar relationship in my kids' lives is the last thing I want for them. Not to mention, I would cause a hell of a setback for myself as I tried to grow out of my childhood wounds.

D = Dispute or Disputing Beliefs. Once I identified the reality of the consequence and possible future consequences, I could write down my disputing beliefs. Had I known these beliefs beforehand, just think of the different result I could have caused and the pain I could've saved everyone involved. As you go through this part of the exercise, you need to know what is the ideal result for the betterment of this situation? What would have been a more ideal event so fewer people would be affected negatively? Once I know these answers, I can build my disputing beliefs around them.

Instead of being insecure about my boys creating a great relationship with their mother, I could choose a new belief—maybe the belief that if I supported them having a deep relationship, it would deepen or strengthen my relationship with them. Maybe my belief was an insecure, jealous fear that pulled us all further away from each other. Logically switching that belief to one that says if we all support each other, we will come out better in the long run is the best-case scenario.

E = Effect. After I pinpointed the belief, I would take a moment and pay attention to the new image or effect I had created in my mind. I would also note the mental and physical state I felt after the process.

For an entire year, I consistently filled out multiple sheets each night —and it always made me feel better each evening I did it.

As I improved in being more conscious of my thoughts, I found I could make far better decisions during new events and moments. At that point, I started filling out far fewer sheets. More importantly, I gradually felt happy as a person.

I was committed to our 3–5-year reprogramming plan and continued seeing Steve until we had reached that goal. Afterward, even though I wasn't filling out the sheets anymore, he helped me stay on track and learn to be accountable.

I.C.E.

I got so great at the A.B.C.D.E. process that I created my own shortcut of it that I call I.C.E. It stands for Identify, Choose, Execute.

I.C.E. works like this; whenever I'd catch myself-feeling elevated about a situation, I'd quickly say to myself, "ICE." That put me on track to: **Identify** my thought; **Choose** a new thought, and **Execute** it. I.C.E. has helped me countless times in many moments over the years. It's probably kept me out of jail more than I know.

Three Big Skills

These two exercises helped me develop three big skills that took my networking game to the next level.

1. **Self-Accountability:** I can now break down and dispute all my initial, hard-wired thoughts as I expose my limited thinking. I can refute the excuses I believed and the justifications I always made. Taking self-accountability forced me to take extreme accountability for my actions and words.

2. **Self-Awareness:** When you consistently practice a method like A.B.C.D.E. or I.C.E., it forces your buried emotions to the surface. When you become aware of them, it gives you the power to control what you couldn't before. When you can control your impulses and actions, you can't stay ignorant. Being aware forces you to operate at a new level—one where you can become a finisher of what you actually set out to do!

3. **Self-Leadership:** When I finally became a leader of myself and didn't allow myself to constantly be sabotaged by my lack of self-control, I improved as a leader in my business and as a leader of others. This enabled me to build stronger teams and a more useful network.

The Power of "What" Versus "Why"

The other helpful exercise Steve and I worked on alongside the A.B.C.D.E method was the power of "What" questions versus "Why" questions.

Whenever I had issues to work through, and would say things to Steve, such as "Why do I keep attracting crazy women?" He would catch me and say, "Kale, why ask why?"

Steve taught me to ask different questions of myself that were more productive. Instead of asking "why," I would turn the question around and say something like: "What am I getting out of dating these women?" Or "What about me makes me keep gravitating to these crazy personalities?"

When you change your questions to challenge yourself and answer why you make the choices you do, it challenges your thinking instead of enforcing a victim mindset.

Did you know that asking "Why me?" is a victim-enforcing term? If our goal is to become more attractive to others and build solid relationships, we must never be sucked into being a victim. I often tell others that a victim mindset or personality is a people repellent that will never help you win in the long run.

I could write an entire chapter on the power of "What" questions versus "Why" questions, but I recently found a brilliant short TED talk by a gal named Tash Eurich. She breaks down telling studies and research on the power of these two questions. I encourage you to check out her talk for a deeper understanding of how you can practice this exercise in your life to encourage productive thinking. Just follow this link: https://bit.ly/TashTED.

The Takeaways That Will Benefit You

The A.B.C.D.E. process and the "What" versus "Why" questions were the two main exercises I implanted into my daily life.

I followed the plan that Steve devised and that these exercises called for, and am living proof that rewiring yourself to think differently, creating a new self-image and personality is not only possible but very achievable.

Shooting for three to five years of reprogramming allows you to see positive results. But I also believe that you will regress at what you stop doing. If you are concerned about maintaining this new way of life, I assure you that when you find a new way of thinking that brings you joy, you will constantly challenge negative ways of thinking.

What's Upcoming

This book will take you through the key areas in business networking that will completely change the trajectory of your business.

You will learn critical strategies for getting more out of your business relationships to take you to the highest levels you want to achieve.

To become an Ultimate Networking Machine, you must become a person people are attracted to, a person they want to be around and who they will trust. By making the ultimate commitment to transform into an elite version of myself, I discovered that my business, by default, flourished as well.

Becoming a person of willingness encouraged me to be honest with myself. I can now seek help, pay my dues and do the work required to become a person of wealth.

Since I've implemented these exercises, I have scaled businesses and investments and continue to do so. This process has taught me that the real secret to monetary wealth is cultivating the right relationships with the right people.

As you do this, you will find that the wealth of happiness and love from others and yourself is by far the most rewarding.

We often hear that money can't buy happiness, but I will argue with anyone that money is a magnifier. It leads to more blessings in your life. If you're willing to do the work required to change your life and make transforming yourself into being a person of willingness, when the money comes, it will magnify all the great areas of your life.

I know from personal experience that If you become willing, you will become wealthy.

CHAPTER 3

SALES IS A FOUNDATION

"To say that a person feels listened to means a lot more than just their ideas get heard. It's a sign of respect. It makes people feel valued."
—Deborah Tannen

One asset that helped me develop into a great networker, a better business owner, and a better leader is my foundation in sales.

In my experience, a foundation in sales is crucial in separating you from your competition.

Even if you're not in sales, you're likely reading this book because you want to get better in your business or networking. Working in sales and committing to understanding it will help you.

Tough Come Up

When I got into sales, I was a nobody with a brand-new child and marriage at the ripe old age of eighteen.

To make ends meet, I'd jumped around from job to job, pushing grocery carts, stocking shelves, slaving away in a Walmart distribution center, and doing construction on the weekends with my dad.

I was a blue-collar worker, trying to get money anywhere I could to feed my family, and if it wasn't for the opportunity to get into sales, I would have probably settled into the labor force. Yes, I would have probably made more money as I rose up the ranks, but I would likely be an employee—a construction worker or hard laborer making between $20-40 bucks an hour.

There's nothing wrong with that plan if it's what you want and it makes you happy.

I didn't want it. It wasn't making me happy.

**Thankfully, sales changed my life.
This is how it happened....**

An Unexpected Turn

I was driving around in my blue P-O-S Honda Accord I'd bought from a friend. Straight up, this car used to be an automatic transmission that was converted to a manual transmission. The kid I bought it from was into racing little burner-type cars. Let's just say… he left his mark on that car, too.

I bought it because I needed a car, and at a couple of thousand bucks, the price was right. It was a pure mode of mobility to get from job one to job two.

This thing had no AC in it, but it did have a heater. But I did not need a heater because I lived in the desert. Even though it got a little cold in the winter, it got very hot in the summer.

Imagine driving around town with your six-month-old baby in the back seat, your wife in the front seat, and it's a scorching 110 degrees.

Then imagine that it gets worse.

To keep the car from overheating, you have to turn on the heat.

My wife and I fought all the time as it was, but add all that irritableness to a 100-degree car with a screaming, sweaty infant, and the annoyance was in a whole new realm. Our son was so young that all he could do was cry from the heat or just fall asleep and try to escape it. His poor little onesies were always damp on his back, and his face would turn beet red.

SALES IS A FOUNDATION

On longer drives, we would frequently stop at gas stations just to cool off and grab some water.

For a while, I was grateful that we even had a car, but as time went on and more parts needed fixing, I couldn't afford the repairs or the new A/C system.

I felt like a failure for putting my little baby and wife through those summers. Then a good twist happened: I got impatient with trying to save.

After crunching the numbers, I found a way to get a better car. I figured from all my paychecks and side jobs that if I could find a car that was only $200 a month, I could swing it.

The only catch was that I needed a $10,000 loan to do it. Thankfully, we finally convinced my wife's grandmother to co-sign. My parents didn't have the credit to help us, and her parents didn't trust us to get a loan together.

With the money secured, I went on the hunt for a new-to-us ride.

At the time, I had my eyes and heart set on a 1998 Toyota Camry. It was slightly used, a few years old, and ten thousand dollars. The Camry was the hottest car at the time for the price and one of the most reliable. They moved very quickly and were hard to find.

After a couple of weeks of hunting for this car, I found one. I connected with the owner, Ryan, who said, "I'll be back in St. George (where I lived) on Monday. If you come and see it, I'll hold this car for you." I had made my mind up to buy this car as soon as I saw it. So, I agreed and went to meet Ryan at an office building.

When I got there, I asked the receptionist, "Is Ryan here?" When she paged him, and he came out, I said, "I'm the kid that called about the car."

He cringed a little and said, "Dude, I'm so sorry. I tried to find your phone number to call you back. I had to sell that car. Someone else called and offered me way over what you and I had talked about. It was a cash deal. I had to take it."

He could see from the look on my face that I was super bummed. Then he offered (I guess to make me feel better), "But I do have a side gig, flipping cars."

I thought, *what in the world does this have to do with me?*

Ignoring the confusion on my face, Ryan explained, "I have a dealer's license and go down to the auction in Las Vegas where I buy popular cars, then flip them to make a few thousand bucks."

I stared at him, rocking on my heels, waiting to find out what the connection of his explanation was to me—but I forced myself to keep my mouth shut until he finished.

"What I'm going to do," he said with a smile replacing his frown, "is cut you a deal. We can pick these cars up at auction for eight grand. If you just roll down there with me, pay me five hundred bucks on whatever we find you, and you have your loan all ready to go, I'll hook you up. It's the least I can do since I sold this car out from under you. That way, you can drive it home. We both win because I don't have to worry about transportation fees."

Now, I was the one smiling. "Damn! It's a deal. When's the next time you're going down there?"

He slapped the desk and said with a big grin, "This weekend!"

We made plans to meet to head to Vegas, and I took off to put in motion what I needed to do to make it happen.

SALES IS A FOUNDATION

With my preapproval in hand, I worked all week, anxious for the day I would meet Ryan.

I met Ryan on the appointed day, and we rode down to Las Vegas with the owner of the business where he worked and another guy who owned a marketing and call center.

These men were obviously more experienced than me, an 18-year-old punk kid. I was a blue-collar labor grunt while these guys made millions of dollars. Even Ryan made several thousand dollars every week at his full-time job—that didn't include what he made at his side gig flipping cars.

I was completely intrigued listening to these guys talk about their business and soaked up their conversation as we drove to the auction. Once we got there, I found and bought a Toyota Camry. Buying it was harder than I thought it would be—people snapped them up!

You had to be on your game in the bidding war and make a decision on the spot, and there wasn't much time to check the engine or anything else on the car. But I finally got a 1998 green Toyota Camry. The color wasn't what I wanted, but it ran well, and the A/C worked like a dream. That's all I wanted for my wife and child at the time.

Once I'd secured the car, Ryan clapped me on the shoulder and said, "It takes a while to process these cars and get them ready to drive home, so let's go grab lunch at the Bellagio."

At the time, the Bellagio was the newest, hottest casino on the strip. I was scared to go because I hadn't budgeted for that kind of lunch! I'd ridden down there with twenty bucks in my pocket, but the casino buffet was forty bucks a head!

As I calculated how I could afford lunch, I broke out in a sweat.

Oh my gosh, *I'm going to have to pull out my twenty and put the rest on my debit card.* I could do it, but it would be super embarrassing. As I weighed the humiliation of what I was about to experience, one of the guys we rode down with ended up buying everybody's lunch. I finally let out the breath I hadn't realized I'd been holding in.

That day, I ate shark, escargot, sushi, and other foods I'd never seen before. The guys I was with just shoveled it in, so I did the same. Some of it was great, some of it not so much—as you can imagine.

After chowing down on our strange lunch, we still had more time to kill. One of the dudes suggested, "Let's go play some hands down in the casino." Just like that, I was embarrassed all over again, feeling intensely out of my environment.

I don't have the money to gamble or lose … was all I could think.

So I sat back and watched these guys gamble $2,000 hands. Sometimes they played two hands with a couple of thousand bucks riding on each of them. There was no way I could compete with that.

My eyes grew big as I tried to be cool, but all the while thought: *if I had even one of those stacks, that would be life-changing money.* Yet these guys didn't miss a beat; I watched all three just *give* their money to the casino. They'd go on runs and get some of it back. But overall, they lost thousands. After that mind-blowing experience, it was time to grab our cars and head back to St. George.

As I drove home in my new green car, my mind raced. What do these guys do? I have to figure it out so I can do it, too.

Throughout the trip, Ryan and his buddies had dropped hints, talking about their call center and how much money their sales guys made. They jabbered on about all the cash their marketing guys made, too.

Transitioning

When I got home, I told my wife, "I want to try doing the sales thing. Walmart is just not for me. And I don't want to work with my dad doing construction forever, either. I know there's something better."

As I pled my case, her face grew pale. I knew what I was up against. My wife was concerned because her father kept selling us on how great Walmart was, all the benefits that would be ours soon. "If you can stick it out, you can earn up to $50,000 a year," he would tell me with a smile. She would never go against her father, but she also knew she had to let me try to do what I felt in my heart—since it was my career. After a couple of weeks of working on her, she agreed to me trying out the sales gig. That was a start, and it was all I needed.

I knew Ryan and the other guys on the trip made legit money. I'd watched them literally gamble sometimes $4,000 at a time. After seeing them pass around that type of money, I had to check it out.

Finally, I called Ryan.

**I've always wanted bigger things.
I've also always known I was meant to do them,
especially when it came to money.**

My whole life, I've loved money and known I was bound for success. After witnessing what I did on the Vegas trip, I did not want to continue limiting myself. Even though I was young, it was impossible to listen to the older people in my life telling me what they thought was best for me.

When I returned to the office building where Ryan worked and walked into the company, it was crazy. Rows of guys in cubicles all paced around, wearing headsets, pitching deals, writing numbers up on the board. I didn't know what any of it meant.

Somewhere in the madness, I found Ryan, who gave me the tour and explained what my job would be. He pointed to a bunch of numbers scribbled on a board, "Whatever you make over here, you earn a commission on. Then you split the deal. There's a setter (which is a prober) and a closer. The model is a two-part sell."

None of what he said made any sense to me … yet. What did make sense was the money on the board and what the reps were boarding—weekly totals of $20,000 and $30,000. I noted the sliding scale for the commission structure and did the math in my head. *Wow, this guy made $5,000 this week. That guy over there made $6,000!*

Almost everybody had money on the board. I figured those who didn't were probably in training, new, or sucked at sales. For the most part, everybody was making $500, $1,000, $2,000, $3,000, even $6,000 in a single week.

As I stared at the numbers, I couldn't wrap my head around them. I remember thinking, wait … are these really their sales for the month? No, these are their sales for the week.

Back home, I talked to my in-laws and wife, insisting, "I can't not try this. If it doesn't work out, I can always go back to another salaried job and work my way up, but I'm still young…. So … I want to try sales."

There was no way I was backing down, not after I was learning how possible it was to make real, life-changing money. My mother-in-law looked straight at me and, without flinching, said, "I don't want you two living with us forever."

That stung.

What stung worse was my father-in-law's expression—a mix of an eye roll and eyebrow raise. "Okay, go on being an idiot then," he said as he walked off.

SALES IS A FOUNDATION

I absorbed what everyone said, and knowing no one could stop me, returned to work even more excited than before.

The company hired me, and I was assigned to a team leader, who handed me some scripts and a printout of their old leads. If you're in sales, you know as the new person, you never get new leads. Those are gold. Instead, he chucked the old leads at me and said, "Here you go!" as he threw me into the water to see if I could swim.

In my cubicle, scared shitless, I made my first call. My sweaty fingers dialed while I hoped that the customer on the other end did not answer—because I did not know what I was doing.

To compound my nervousness, I was also a horrible reader. I'd dropped out of high school, having never been that great at it. I wasn't the kid who went home and studied often, so naturally, I sucked at reading. That day, it felt like I could *barely* read. As I struggled through the script, I sounded like a robot, just parroting off the words to these old leads.

Eventually, someone listened to my painful probing. I was through the first level!

But there was more.

Once you got through the initial probe, you had to ask personal information. I needed to know how much money was available on their credit cards, if they were married, if their spouse could get on the phone, if they had any money in savings, and so on. It was highly uncomfortable as I forced myself to ask about their intimate information.

But I did it.

Over and over and over again.

After enough calls, I walked my first probe over to the closer. He looked up at me and sniped, "This better be good, and you better not waste my time. I don't want to hear at the end of the call that this guy's credit cards are maxed out." I know he was just covering his ass and going over the stuff the closers typically went through with the trainees, but what an asshat. As I walked away to return to my tiny cubicle, I worried I would let him down.

The joke was on him because he actually closed the deal—which meant I got paid, too!

My First Lead ... My First House

My new client bought a $6,000 marketing package; the closer boarded $3,000 of it, and I boarded $3,000.

From that one phone call, I'd made a fast $500. And it was my first week on the phone! That commission paid me what I would have made in an entire week, both from working at the Walmart Distribution Center and working for my dad.

I was hooked.

Every week I got a little bit better.

Before long, I was making $1,000, $1,500, and on a great week—I even made $2,000.

After working that job for three or four months, at not even nineteen years old, I could buy my first house.

Granted, buying a house in the early 2000s wasn't as complicated or challenging as it is today. We didn't have to jump through all the hoops to get a loan. Bankers handed them out like Halloween candy. I still had an advantage when it was time to buy since I could provide a stated income loan and pay stubs to back it up. Within five months of taking that job, I closed on a home for $150,000. And my life completely changed.

Chapter 4

THE CLOSER CULTURE

"Great salespeople are relationship builders, who provide value and help their customers win."
—Jeffrey Gitomer

Before long, I'd bought into the sales culture and the rush of getting a deal done. Then I had my eye on moving up and becoming a closer. I paid very close attention to what closers said and did and made it my mission to ask questions so that I could get to that level. I know I drove some of the closers crazy, asking them about the psychology of the sell, analyzing the tonality and fluctuations of the prospects' voices. I'd ask about positions for the close, assuming the sale, what they would do after they got the payment, the process of contracting the client, etc.

Closers made $4,000-5,000 a week, and the better ones made an unbelievable $6,000. After working tirelessly and learning everything I could about being a closer, I was ready to go after that position.

As I moved up, I learned some great strategies for becoming a great networker in sales that everybody can benefit from. The first tip was how to relate to people by being chameleon-like.

If I could relate to people, then I could more easily earn their trust. In sales, you must build rapport, gain trust, and become likable to your customer. Learning this has served me well in my business as a networker for years. Getting people to trust you enough so they will refer their clients to you isn't easy. But if you master this skill, it will help you build your sales foundation.

> **I also learned how to use a prospect's goals, ambitions, and desires as selling points. When I paid attention, I could persuade people.**

The more I sold, the more I realized that becoming a better listener is one of the most powerful actions you can take as a sales professional. As I got better and better, I also learned how to change my attitude and personality in an instant when I needed to.

On those days when I wasn't feeling all sunshine and rainbows, I could still turn it on and force it out, so I was more appealing to our prospects and clients.

The strategies I learned from this job were priceless.

In addition to figuring out what to do as a business operator, I also figured out what not to do. Unlearning was necessary to grow myself to new levels.

The Wrong Way

What people were practicing at this company wasn't on the up and up. It became more apparent that if I was going to keep improving in sales, I needed to leave behind the shadier aspects of sales like focusing on the cash grab, getting the sale at any cost, using unethical word crafting, letting the prospects believe that "guarantee" meant the same as "service warranty," and preying on the desperation of people. I wouldn't do it at this company or even the one after it, but while people insisted these ways were okay, and I practiced them, I didn't feel good about them. When I launched my second company, that's when I changed the way I sold forever. But for now, I just kept at it, doing what I could to get those dollars on the board.

If you are using any of these frowned-upon tactics, please stop. Taking part in what might be perceived as manipulative sales tactics and selling products to people who aren't going to benefit from them, as well as selling products you don't believe in or that don't make a positive impact in someone's life, will stunt your growth.

I wouldn't be where I've gotten to in my career in these last ten years if I had continued the course I was on for the first five years. So if you see yourself here, you can make these changes and shorten your gaps in leveling up.

Implementing better sales tactics took some hard lessons of getting merchant accounts closed, money frozen, and dealing with cancels and chargebacks from unhappy customers. Trying to take shortcuts caused an endless cycle of having to sell more to keep our heads above water to survive.

For the past 10 years, we stayed in an upright cycle. We built our processes to provide higher quality service that begins from the sales call. We want customers to have a pleasing experience.

Sure, you can make a lot of sales with high-pressure sales tactics, but you will never keep customers if your business model centers around the cash grab. It's only a matter of time until you will crash and burn, too.

In my business now, we focus on making the sale, but more importantly, we want to create an awesome experience—that byproduct is usually another sale.

Saying your company or service is the best is fine, but other people saying that you're the best is the most powerful sales strategy ever.

Combining Sales Tactics with Networking

I still love the art of persuasion, building rapport, and listening with intent as I feel the rush of closing a big deal.

You must possess those skills to be a great networker as well because even though you're networking, you still need to be a closer.

Remember, we want business and key relationships to come to us. Building a solid reputation will make you magnetic. More importantly, you will feel proud of yourself when you run business the right way.

One of the best things you can do to compound growth and scale your business is sell something you believe in that will positively affect a person's life. Do this, and your clients will want to tell other people about their experience and your product.

It seems like a no-brainer, but most small businesses don't focus on what the buyer is feeling. In turn, their business gets stuck in that "churn and burn" model—they're always chasing the next sale.

My questions to you are:

What are your sales tactics?

Are you really proud of how you sell?

If so, that's great! If not, you may need to tap into your willingness and make some hard adjustments. Most likely, you're just not listening to that deep truth in the back of your mind because you know it is going to take massive effort to change. It's time to become willing to do that.

Yes, it means stepping back, taking pay cuts, and rebuilding steps and processes that don't seem logical at times, but are you willing to do it for the greater good?

If you are, your ceiling just got a lot higher. Your potential just maximized.

How willing you are will determine your future.

CHAPTER 5

MORE MONEY, MORE OPPORTUNITY

"Problems are opportunities, and conquered opportunities equal money earned."
—Grant Cardone

There are so many moving parts to money and fully understanding it is overwhelming to most business owners.

However, you must get an immediate understanding of the basics at every level when you are a business owner. If you do not have a strategic and a tactical plan for your money, you are doomed!

I truly think it's not if you're going to fail but when if you don't know the elementary rules. I know that sounds harsh, but I've lived on both sides of the money lows and highs.

Take my father, for instance. Some of the values I learned from him I wanted to apply in my life, some I knew I should not apply.

My dad is a hard worker to this day. He's in his mid-sixties and still owns a construction business. He packs up ladders and hauls them around to job sites, jumps up in lifts, crawls through tight spots, and does other tasks that he probably shouldn't be doing much longer.

Even though he has a crew, he's the one hopping up to do the work. I love that he is such a hard worker and that he instilled a hard work ethic into me. But I have also learned from him what financial habits not to adopt.

Although I admire how hard he's worked his whole life and the importance of having a strong ethic, there is also a ton of value in learning to work smarter, but not always harder. Yes, you can work hard in certain areas where it makes sense, but to really create wealth, you must get your money to work for you.

Young Money

I had a mindset shift young. At a very early age, I made the choice that I was going to be rich. I was not going to have the same financial struggles that my father dealt with in his life and business. I remember thinking as a young adult and working for my dad, *why would anybody want to be a business owner? Why would anybody want to work this hard just so the IRS can come and take it away?*

That's exactly what happened to my dad. He worked his butt off, but he was horrible at watching his money. He didn't keep records. He paid his bills, but not his taxes. He never knew what to pay, how much, or when to pay what he owed.

Unfortunately, he is not the only one. It's very common for business owners to wing it when it comes to their money. I see it every day at EASIER ACCOUNTING.

These business owners have no idea how much doing this is hurting them and holding them back in so many areas.

As I embarked on my career path, I've found that most entrepreneurs avoid this area. Nobody wants to pay taxes. It's the least fun thing to do in business. People don't want to do their record keeping. They don't want to meet with their bookkeeper or tax preparer, planner, or financial expert once a month. They want to focus on what brings in the money—where it is going.

> **Taxes will always be one of your highest expenses unless you do something about it.**

I was lucky enough to have a brilliant moment that stayed with me and taught me—that I learned through my dad. I know I do not want to be a person who has everything taken away. My dad had a lien on his home, and his bank accounts levied.

My mom had to get a job, although her paychecks were garnished by the IRS. They were both forced into bankruptcy.

A business that works for cash under the table has it tough. When you can't take on customers that want to pay by check or credit, it puts a strain on your sales. I saw this exact non-strategy cripple my dad's business. Then I watched as it, in part, crippled my parents' marriage and our home life.

> **About 90% of the fights in our home between my mom and dad revolved around money. Maybe you can relate to that. It's a reality for so many people.**

After living through a financially torn household, I made up my mind at a tender age that I was not going to live the same way. I was going to be rich!

I remember stating just that to one of our neighborhood church leaders. We grew up in a Mormon community where the church assigned visiting teachers to pop in and check on their assigned families.

One day, our teacher came over to check in and share a quick lesson. Before he left, he asked me, "What do you want to be when you grow up?"

I was only around seven or eight years old, but I can distinctly recall looking into his face and declaring, "I want to be a millionaire, and I'm going to be one."

The teacher laughed at me.

He said, "That's fine and dandy, but what are you going to *do* to become a millionaire?"

I shrugged back at him.

I didn't know.

I just knew I wanted to be one.

As a small child, I knew money was important.

Luckily, I got into sales and absorbed what I could about making money. Then thankfully, I realized quickly that I wasn't going to become wealthy by being just a salesman.

You can make a lot of money in sales, but in the companies I sold for, I saw limitations. They capped you out at $100,000 a year, and the amount of wealth that I wanted to create wasn't going to come from that kind of money. I wanted to be an investor and businessman!

Introduction to Accounting

My sales ability developed from my years of being a salesman, and that led me to a man who owned a tax and accounting company. He did a presentation for all the sales guys where I worked as a 1099 rep in that first call center job, and I learned he was looking for a salesman. At that time, the company I was selling for was going through some transitions that made me insecure about my future there.

After the presentation, I talked to the owner of the tax and accounting company. He told me all about how you can save money on taxes and the different write-offs available to independent contractors and self-employed operators.

I really liked his presentation and him. So, when I found out his company was hiring for a sales position, I jumped on the opportunity to work for him.

After a few years, I became very skilled at selling tax and accounting services and speaking to business owners. That's when I realized that more than anything, I wanted to be my own boss. Based off what I'd learned, it didn't seem like the taxes were that scary. For business owners, the tax code is simply a guide as to where to invest your money and get it working for you, all while creating tax deductions and utilizing every benefit you can.

After structuring my taxes correctly, I learned I was at an advantage and able to keep more of my money while putting it to work for me.

But there was a catch…. Even though I had that knowledge, I couldn't apply it yet because I was working for somebody else.

Chapter 6

TAKING THE LEAP

*"To build a successful business,
you must start small and dream big."*
—Aliko Dangote

It was time to start my first side business—and surprisingly, it wouldn't be in accounting. I embarked on trading currency online and joined forces with my friend Jeremy—who's still my partner to this day—all while continuing to work my main job.

One of the greatest gifts ever given to me was my boss at the call center finding out about my new business. To my mind, I didn't have anything to hide from him. And I was very honest with him about what I was doing. It would have been impossible to hide anyway; I was so excited about it.

When I approached him, I said, "This is my new gig I am doing after hours, and I can see the potential. There's even a possibility to refer clients here to your company." He didn't say much, and I didn't think anything of it, so I just went back to work.

About a week after our discussion, he pulled me into his office and let me go. His parting words were: "Maybe you'll thank me one day."

Of course, I didn't think him firing me was a great development at the time, and I sure as hell didn't feel like thanking him.

I was scared.

In that moment, I lost a six-figure job because of my business that wasn't even turning a profit yet.

> **Luckily, I had paid attention to how my boss operated his business. So, I'd learned a lot of effective skills and ideas to use in my new business, as well as what not to use.**

Like any entrepreneur, I had some brilliant moments, and I had some smart moments.

Of course, I also had some dumb moments; thankfully, I had learned enough to recover quickly.

With no full-time job, I had to succeed. There was no choice. So, I went all in.

Instantly, my take-home was massively slashed. The lifestyle I'd created from making six figures was a far cry from what I was making at my new business.

If my new company was going to take off, I had to create better money habits. Like yesterday.

Everything I had ever wanted was coming true. I was finally in a position to execute the choice I'd made in my life when I was a child. I could immerse myself in my business at last. Accompanied by the tax knowledge I'd accrued from years of working at a tax and accounting firm, I was ready. We had a scalable business, and I had the ambition, motivation, and work ethic to create a little success.

A few successes became more successes.

Scaling

Eventually, we scaled our business to a $2 million-dollar company. Teaching people how to trade currency online was lucrative.

Then right in the middle of grabbing all that momentum, the federal government assigned the NFA (National Futures Association) to step in and regulate the Forex market. We found ourselves lacking. We didn't have a Series 7 or all the licenses required to advise people as to what to do with their money in Forex.

Gone was our ability to make kickbacks from the brokerages. To give you a frame of reference, the crazy volatility is like what the crypto market went through in early 2022.

Since the market had been unregulated for a while, people were making and losing millions. The government tried to get its share by figuring out ways to regulate it.

That curveball changed the game for us. We could sell our course, but I knew that opportunity would dwindle quickly—and it did.

Getting Accountable

It was time to pivot. I loved the tax and accounting industry and was passionate about it from having been brought up in a home with severe tax and financial struggles. I also loved helping business owners start off on the right foot.

That was all the motivation I needed to start my own tax and accounting company.

Jeremy and I partnered up with a couple of more friends who had also worked at the old company and quickly launched our own firm.

We scaled that company to over $10 million within a couple of years. I learned I was quite skilled in growing our company and selling tax and accounting services to business owners, especially startup owners. People in those initial phases don't understand much about what they need to do to start off on the right foot. Helping them do this saves them thousands and thousands of dollars in the long run.

The majority of businesses that fail do so because of some financial issue. Taxes, poor accounting, no accounting (like my dad practiced), lack of funding, or not enough capital to sustain themselves, etc., are all reasons businesses fold.

Business owners get themselves into a financial bind or tax trouble, and that trouble compounds until they're in a hole they can't dig themselves out of.

After several years of running our tax and accounting company, a couple of our partners decided to spin-off and create their own business. They wanted more ownership and fewer partners. Unfortunately, they were a little sneaky about it. I found out some embezzling was going on—which was another lesson for me to always watch your money properly. I had no idea funds were disappearing. I could have sued my former partners, but I don't like to waste my money in court systems. I don't like to waste my time fighting. That's senseless to me when I can make money with my time.

Instead of suing them, I moved forward with a new tax and accounting company alongside new partners.

As I ran our business, I learned a critical financial habit that you must apply to your business to create wealth. You are not going to save yourself into wealth. It requires investing.

Building wealth is hard to do when you have no knowledge of how money works.

Nine out of 10 business owners don't understand taxes, tax reduction, proper accounting, investing back into their business, outside investments, passive income, active income, interest income, and more. Nor do they want to know. Again, they have no idea what it's really costing them.

Even though the wealthiest people on this planet will openly tell you that to create wealth, you first must practice healthy financial habits, people who want to create wealth but remain broke still don't act.

Money is a tool—one that you need to scale and grow at every level.

Three Biggest Money Mistakes Business Owners Make

Business owners make a lot of money mistakes, but these are the three most costly ones you want to avoid:

1. **They Live Beyond Their Means**: While you're building a business, you must have reserves built up specifically for the business. Unfortunately, most business owners won't sacrifice the possessions and stuff they want right now for a brighter future. Instead, they inch their lifestyles up until they're barely keeping their head above water. Then when an unforeseen issue arises (usually sooner than later), they can't cover payroll, payments, rents, product cost, etc.

   In all the businesses I have been a part of, I made sure that my partners and I all agreed with a specific amount to keep in reserves. We do this before we even advertise. It's not fun! We also realized we had to pay taxes on those dollars even though we couldn't take the money personally. That wasn't a party either. However, doing this has allowed us to stay alive in downtimes and make sizable reinvestments into the growth of the business when we are more affluent.

   Opportunity always seems to find money, so you better have some!

2. **They Avoid Early Tax Planning**: No one loves paying taxes (not anyone who I've met anyway). You might think because a business owner would want to be prepared that they would look forward to it, but they don't.

Most avoid it. They procrastinate all year, dreading tax time because they follow the typical broken system of filing taxes at the last minute and overpaying in several ways. That's nerve-wracking and panic-inducing! Why put yourself through that?

An early-in-the-year plan with quarterly 30-minute check-ins is so valuable. It gives people a plan to follow all year, ensuring mistakes aren't made and deductions aren't missed. When you take these steps, it saves you a ton of time and stress when it's time to file.

A proper initial tax plan involves a review of previous taxes (if it's your first year with a new tax professional).

This review allows your tax professional to identify any mistakes that were made or adjustments that could be made to reduce taxes. It also allows them to see how your business is structured so you can build a new plan around that business structure.

You would be surprised at how much money you can put back in your pocket simply by using the right structure. So many people set up an LLC or corporation based on bad advice. They don't realize what it costs them.

You may need an S corporation and nine LLCs like I currently have. You may need a C corporation or one single-member LLC. Your choice needs to be customized to your needs so you can flow your money properly through your structure and maximize all the deductions you are legally eligible for.

Some specific rules and tax strategies that you can do through an S corporation you can't do through a single-member LLC and vice versa. When we plan around the third part of a plan—the tax reduction section—it's important to make sure you're set up properly for the most gain.

We recently had a doctor call us specifically for our tax plan service. She knew something was off with her taxes and needed a second opinion.

After one discovery call and analyzing her past returns, we found she was overpaying her taxes by over $40,000—and not just in that one year! She had overpaid by this amount every year. Her plan was extensive because she has multiple properties, investments, a medical practice, and her husband's business dealings.

She paid us just over $10,000 for the plan and to restructure her reporting. But the whole mess could have been avoided if she'd have been properly structured earlier on.

We did amend her returns and not only got her the $40,000 back for two previous years, but we also set her up to avoid overpaying each year moving forward. I'd say that's quite an investment, wouldn't you?

A proper plan set early in the year will save you money and sanity.

3. **They Use the Wrong Accounting Team**: I'll make this quick. Our system is backward, and that's how the IRS likes it.

   There are billions of overpaid tax dollars each year. Most of our clients come to us because they are sick of the once-a-year tax pro that never picks up their calls or returns calls.

   You need an accountant who works for you, who does not work for the IRS.

   No matter who you hire for accounting, check their systems and processes. A great firm will have mandatory systems and processes to deliver your numbers on time each month,

   Their processes are built to help hold you accountable to get them your information each month or quarter—so they can take it off your hands.

A great firm will also commit you to do your part so they can do their part. We tell our new customers that we expect to be fired if we don't do our part, but we will also fire them as a client if they don't do theirs.

Having effective mandatory systems and processes and a team that is there for you throughout the year allows you to keep much more of your profits versus throwing them away. A plan allows you to avoid ignorance and impulsive financial moves.

Ignorance + Impulsiveness = Implosion.

This really is a tricky part of business, but it can also be so simple. It's tricky because most business owners love making and using money but can't stand learning about it.

If you are someone who can relate to that, you need to get a financial person or team around you to get you out of that routine. It is an investment, not an expense.

Right now, your ignorance and impulsive decisions are an expense.

Having a great accounting team will help you avoid many costly issues. The investment far outweighs the cost of your ignorance and impulsiveness.

If you're willing to do your part in utilizing a team by checking in monthly and consulting with them before you buy things in your business, it is absolutely an investment. It will allow you to keep running your business without feeling like you are all alone and have to learn about money by yourself.

Having a team will also put you in a position to grow your network. That's one of the biggest and most valuable points I want to leave you with in this chapter.

CHAPTER 7

THE MAGIC FORMULA OF WEALTH AND NETWORKING

"The rich invest in time. The poor invest in money."
—*Warren Buffett*

Building wealth has everything to do with networking. There are benefits to having wealth and savings, getting liquid, and building valuable relationships that will help you grow your business.

I wouldn't have any of my investments if it weren't for my ability to invest to be in the right rooms and climb the ladder of networking. I also wouldn't have some of my referral partners if I hadn't been able to beat out my competitors.

I bested them by investing in businesses that became my affiliate and referral partners, by cultivating my business relationships.

One gentleman was looking for investors to fund the launch of his software, so he could help business owners. He's in the B2B market. Naturally, I want to work with people who are in this market so they can refer business owners to my accounting firm.

I like helping business owners win when it comes to their finances and tax experience. When business owners put money back in their pockets, it's almost like an insurance policy they can depend on when things don't go right (and it's properly deducted). I've assembled a team over the years that can do that because helping businesses owners avoid financial issues has become a passion of mine.

Establishing insurance accounts for business owners to recoup or re-invest is one of our most rewarding strategies.

I love being a solution to small business owners who want to launch their business correctly. I get to help them avoid financial turmoil in their homes. That's payback for me for what I saw in my family. I don't like seeing small business owners struggle so hard that it rips their families and homes apart. Money ignorance can be solved so easily.

Putting My Money Where My Mouth is

I wouldn't have the valuable relationships I have now if I wasn't willing to get my money right myself.

A big part of my networking strategy now is investing in the most expensive masterminds and business clubs. I view it as an investment because of the returns it has brought into our businesses and the lives of others within our businesses. It's hard for people to see the extent of these rewards until they have experienced it for themselves, but it's really quite simple.

If you're paying a higher price to be around a bunch of other people paying that higher price, you're paying to surround yourself with people at higher levels than the average business person. Each one of those people also has higher-level networks that you now have an opportunity to tap into. This is how I have built the majority of my referral partners.

Seventy-five percent of our business revenue comes from referral partners. Since we've been able to build to an 8-figure business, our network has been pretty valuable to us.

We had to have money to get in these networks, and that called for establishing early reserves. This put us in a position to scale when opportunity came knocking. When we had a desired referral partner considering us versus a competitor, we invested heavily to influence his decision to work with us.

This is just one example of how we have reacted quickly and invested serious cash to change the outcome to one we desired.

Our referral partner was already working with a competitor, but he decided to build a new expensive software to service his clients better. He wanted to bring on investors for the software build. Keep in mind his clients are ideal clients for us as well.

So, after a round of golf and learning that his current firm was not willing to be an investor in his project, we swooped in for the kill. As we hung out on the ninth hole, I mentioned. "You know my partners, and I really believe in you and your product. We'd like to invest $50,000, so you can meet your funding goals and get to work. Can we make that happen?" The smile that broke out across his face gave me my answer.

I knew that having his business referrals would make our investment back in less than three months. Even if his software never produced a return, I couldn't lose.

This example is not uncommon for us; we have loaned and invested money several times to beat out competitors. Understand we could never be in that position without the strategy of big sacrifices for big reserves in our businesses. The sooner you remember that money is a tool and you get smart with it, the sooner you can use that tool to be an ultimate networker in your business.

Our track record speaks for itself. Because our affiliate partners know we could easily go to their competitors, they choose to work with our company.

Investing in a person in this way gives me the opportunity to build a relationship with them.

When you take a chance on people, people will take a chance on you.

When you believe in somebody and their vision and mission, it not only helps them trust you and give you their business, but it makes them like you.

Think about the people you like in your life.
Probably, these are the people who believe in you.
They are the people who lift you up.
They're willing to invest their time, money, and energy into you.

How can you play ball at that level of business to build those types of relationships if you don't have the money to get in the game with them? If you don't have the money to take a chance on them?

I hope you see the value in having enough financial freedom, liquidity, and financial stability, to invest with the people with who you want to scale and grow your business—your referral partners.

People are the Real Reward

One of the most important parts of your network is the people who send you business. It's not easy for a lot of business owners to do because their customers are valuable to them. They don't want to send them to a business they don't have any faith in.

This is why making sacrifices is essential in the beginning. Material items that don't make you money can be given up. The non-essentials you think you want can stand in the way of building up liquidity in your life and business. Learn to go without so you can take chances with people who are worth it.

I've brought my business a long way just hustling and grinding, putting myself out there, and being present in all the rooms—from the $50 rooms to the $100,000 rooms. I worked my way up.

Once you get in these rooms, make it your goal to get around people with who you desire to do business. I'm talking about people who are at the level you want to be. You have to get in the game with them.

If you're just starting out, like I was when we launched the Forex company, you need to figure out where to cut the non-essential expenses out of your life. While you're sacrificing what you don't need, give yourself an hour every month to design and stick to a budget. Every dollar that you can put away right now is power for you to scale in the future.

Understand the importance of diversification as well. You don't want a million bucks to merely sit there. Invest it with people to earn their business, have money in the markets so you can build compound interest. Make it an aim to understand the different investments that are tax-deductible or depreciable.

Start on the Right Foot

Your first step is to build a financial team. I don't mean hiring an accountant in-house to work for you right away. Even an entry-level accountant fresh out of school will be $15-20/hour, maybe more, depending on where you live. On top of that, there are payroll taxes. Now, add on benefits if you are offering them. After you add everything up, you're talking about an employee who will cost you $3,000-5,000 a month—again, for a full-time entry-level accountant.

That doesn't make sense.

That's the beautiful advantage of outsourcing. It's why I built an outsourced accounting company inside a model with systems and processes that help business owners hold themselves accountable. Don't scrimp here. Doing this will give you the tools needed to help you create wealth, and understand your money, so you know where it's at—which will assist you in making better decisions in your business.

Whether it's investing in building your network, the financial markets for future freedom, or real estate, just make sure you invest.

I'm currently considering a real estate deal with a man I want to do more business with. If we become partners on a few multifamily or single-family deals, they will tie me to him. The more I'm tied to him, the more he gets to know me, the more he will want to do business with me.

Outsourcing with the right company, whether through my business or another, will save you money—but it's got to be the right type of company. If you're going to outsource the accounting, or financial services of your business, for example, you need to align your team. It's crucial that you don't just hire anybody. You need more than someone to do your books for you every month; it's a starting point, but the ideal person for this role has passionately created their systems and processes to care enough about business owners to help hold them accountable. They need to get you what you require on time every month and to conduct calls every single month to intimately understand your money.

I've spoken at events about financial habits, accounting, and understanding your money. Every single time I walk out on that stage, I ask people to raise their hands if they know somebody in their sixties, seventies, or eighties who still has to work to get by. Almost every single person at every single event has raised their hand.

Why?

Because people want to naturally avoid this sector of their business with the least desirable duties. It's not the most fun bill to pay. It's the least sexy part of business.

If you asked people between the ages of 60-80, what they wished they would have done differently, you'll hear: "I wish I would've kept to a budget. I wish I would've hired financial experts who actually cared about my future."

Another question that I always ask from the stage is: "How many people would rather spend 10 or 15 minutes a month on the phone with their outsourced accountant, or financial team, versus 30 to 50-plus hours at the end of the year, scrambling to get their mess put together for their CPA. Remember, when you do this, you're paying the tax preparer more because it's more work for them to go through and plug in all your messy data. If you're not a CPA, a tax expert, or you don't understand money that well, and you're not meeting with your accountant every single month, how much money do you think you're leaving on the table? Ask yourself that question and be honest about the answer.

Then ask yourself this question: if I executed a tax plan ahead of time and followed it throughout the year, spending 15 to 20 minutes a month on the phone with my accounting and financial team, how much money would I save versus overpaying? Further, how much money would that equate to over a few years that I could invest into my network, financial future, or real estate deals with people I want to do business with?

Wrap your mind around the value of having enough money to get in the game.

I'm not going to lie; it will take a sacrifice upfront to get to that level; it will take a bit of investing into your financial team versus avoiding your numbers and taxes—but it will also be worth your peace of mind.

Are you willing to live below your means early on to have money for opportunity?

Are you willing to invest in your network?

Are you willing to plan early, so the above is possible?

Consider these key questions. The sooner you do, the sooner you will get where you want to go.

CHAPTER 8

THE HARD CUTS THAT NEED TO HAPPEN

"Mindlessly going through the motions without improvement can be its own form of suffering."
—Angela Duckworth

Improving your environment will make a huge difference in your life and especially in your business. Your environment makes up the places where you spend your time with the people you allow into your life. It plays a bigger role than you probably think.

A major point of this book is to attract the right people to you. To do that, you have to make some hard cuts on some of the people and places in your life.

When you do this, you will allow the people that you want to come in.

I get asked quite a bit, "How do I know who these people are? And how do I start taking the steps to do this?" I always respond, "Just start paying attention." Pay attention to yourself, pay attention to your habits, pay attention to the places you go and how it makes you feel.

Do you feel like you're getting your worth when you're hanging out in a bar? Do you feel like you're getting your worth when you go to work every day surrounded by drug addicts or people who live lifestyles beneath you?

As you get honest about the people whose company is not serving you, pay attention to people who try to put limitations on you. They are the ones who need to go first. Unfortunately, this is not easy. Most of the time, the people closest to you are the people doing the most harm, so it's the most difficult to let those people out of your life.

> **As humans, we put limitations on ourselves.**
> **We beat ourselves up enough. We're our biggest critics.**
> **Obviously, we don't need anyone else reinforcing that.**

We're already battling ourselves into new directions and habits, into developing deeper convictions about our goals. You simply don't have room for the people trying to put limitations on you.

But Who Needs to Go?

If the people closest to you lift you up or drag you down, if they highlight you in a negative way or make digs at you, goodbye! You may have seen memes on social media saying things like: "Don't speak your goals and dreams to others. Just do the work yourself. Those outside influences are never going to do the work for you or celebrate you."

I think a little bit differently. There's a lot of power in speaking what you really want, what you're going to do, and what your dreams and aspirations are. It's important to speak what you aspire to do into the world because it will expose the people who do try and lift you up, who do cheer you on and celebrate and highlight you—versus the people who want to tear you down.

Maybe you've heard some of these ball busters when it comes to building your business?

"You're not going to build a multi-million-dollar business."

"You better have a backup plan."

"Do you even know where to start?"

THE HARD CUTS THAT NEED TO HAPPEN

"You don't know anything about that industry."

"Who's going to work for you?"

Anyone who is saying things like this to you, cut.

Sometimes these people believe they are speaking out to help you. This "advice" might come from your mother or father. You might get it from your closest relatives and friends when they say, "Make sure you have a plan B," or "Don't quit your job while you're chasing this dream," or "Get your ducks in a row before you do anything because this might not work out for you." They might simply tell you, "Just be careful."

I won't deny that sometimes people have your best interests at heart, but they also don't understand you and what you need in your life. How can they when they're not doing what you want to do?

Almost every business owner, high-level entrepreneur, intrapreneur, and leader I know has realized when their environments needed changing. People are connected to the places we frequent.

I made so many hard cuts for long periods of time in my life. My siblings, my parents, and even my childhood best friend. Some are back in my life now as they made great improvements and now respect my boundaries. But honestly, one of the most inspiring people I've watched change their environment is my best friend and business partner.

Trevor

Trevor is one of my longest-standing business partners. He's also a co-host with me on *The Real Business Owners* podcast, as well as he is a partner in almost all my business ventures. But he had to make some very hard cuts in his life to get to where he's at.

Trevor and I worked together when we were just young kids in the call center space. That's where we met. I gravitated to him because I loved his energy. He was fun and funny, and he gravitated toward me as well.

Even though we are different in many ways, we have very similar beliefs and are both competitors and natural leaders.

I truly think we were matched by God to do some big things together. The combination of us is what has allowed our podcast to reach the top 1% of business podcasts.

We also both have the same heart when it comes to giving and serving people around us.

Trevor and I hit it off quickly and became friends. Then we started hanging out after work. He was only 18, and I was only 19. I already had a child, so I couldn't go out and party with him like I wanted to. I needed to be with my kid. The paycheck I had to bring home was different than the paycheck Trevor needed.

In our sales departments, a lot of guys made good money selling high ticket products. Some guys made several thousand dollars a week, and some only netted $500-1,000. What you made depended on your sales and how hard you worked.

Because Trevor was young, single, and the life of the party, he wanted to hang with people in the company who had habits that didn't serve him. That's when he fell into a new lifestyle. Spend enough time with any person, good or bad, and you will fall into their habits.

Trevor was slowly introduced to pain pills that many guys in the industry were popping. Before long, he went from doing pain pills to heroin.

So, Trevor had to exit my life. I was raising a family. I wasn't going down destructive roads. I was moving into other sales positions at different companies, and so was he—but we were coming from different directions.

THE HARD CUTS THAT NEED TO HAPPEN

Before long, we both left the company where our friendship began. Things had gotten bad for him—he had been doing heroin for years at that point, but Trevor didn't change his environment. He went to other call centers with the same type of people. His addiction got worse.

After about four years of Trevor being a full-time heroin addict and losing everything, he had to make a hard decision. There was nothing left of his life. It was up to him to change his environment and get clean. If he didn't, what he had lost could be gone forever. His mother, stepdad, brother, and sisters told him to go.

Suddenly, he was about to be homeless. That's when his situation got real. His mother sat him down and said, "The only way you can stay here is if you get help—then we can help you get help."

That did it. Trevor kicked heroin. It was a good first step, but he still worked in the call centers and was around some of the same people he needed to cut out of his life. Even if he wasn't doing drugs, he was going out with people who were still drinking. Everyone would go to the bars. They'd mingle after work. So, Trevor started drinking a little more. Eventually, he replaced one bad habit with another one.

Sure, he was more functional when he was using alcohol after hours versus heroin. But he still wound up with a few DUIs on his driving record. That forced him to change his environment again.

Four years later, Trevor and I reconnected when he came to work for me.

I was totally excited to have him come on board with our team because he is an asset with a great personality. Trevor possesses natural leadership qualities. It was more than the fact he was my friend and that we had a history together. I enjoyed being around him and knew he would be a tremendous addition who would work hard and do a lot for our company.

When he started working in the company, we were both overweight drinkers. I didn't drink as much as him because I had a family that I had to come home to every night. So, I didn't go out after work. But on the weekends and during events, we would put it down.

Our call center environment still had certain people we shouldn't have been around—who shouldn't have even worked there.

For a couple of years, Trevor worked with me and kept his addictions under control, but then our situation changed. My business partner, Robert, wasn't working out, and we had to cut ties. He wanted Trevor to work for him when he left—since he had brought Trevor back into the company that we tried to start together. However, I wanted Trevor to stay and work with us.

I told Trevor I wanted him to stay on and be a leader. He was just better at certain things than me. I was anti-confrontational and had a hard time holding employees accountable and having hard conversations with them. Trevor was naturally good at that and could argue with the best of them. He was so good at confrontations that by the end of a conversation, he would build the person up—all while holding them accountable. It's a true art of his! I needed someone who could lead in those areas because I was a pushover.

Maybe it was selfish of me, but I told Trevor I wanted him to turn down Robert, so I could make him a leader. That's exactly what happened.

We started cleaning things up in the company. We instituted random drug tests and fired the people who didn't need to be there.

We now don't have people working in our company that we feel we have to give random drug tests to. Trevor's leadership skills have continued to grow. I started bringing him to events with me, and we got into personal development together. Along the way, I watched Trevor slowly

THE HARD CUTS THAT NEED TO HAPPEN

cut certain people out of his life who couldn't beat their addictions as he had. He wanted to grow.

Eventually, Trevor had his own wife and child. Even though he was miles away from his issues, I still noticed people trying to suck him back down into their world. They called him when they were in jail and needed to be bailed out. They called him when they needed a loan. They called him when they needed a place to stay. Certain people got what they wanted. He allowed them to crash at his family's home until they got back on their feet.

Thankfully, Trevor slowly realized that certain people were trying to pull him down and weren't adding to his life. They weren't lifting him up.

He had hard conversations with his friends and told them, "You're not welcome in my home anymore." "I can't borrow you money." "I can't put a rental car in my name for you."

He established boundaries and not only stopped going to bars and other places where these types of people hung out, but he stopped taking their phone calls after having those hard conversations with them.

Trevor's story is an example of what needs to happen if you want to level up. For him to continue his trajectory of changing his life and making moves—going from six to seven to eight figures, enhancing his personal life, deepening his relationships with his wife and children with his business partners and the people around him, he had to make more room for better people and better environments.

I didn't have addictions or drug problems, and I often say that my son was my savior. If I hadn't had my son, who I love with all my heart, at such a young age, I might have traveled those same roads as well.

While my problems weren't identical to Trevor's, I did have to remove many people from my life who were my triggers.

The People I Cut

My brother was a drug addict, so he had to go. My sister and I got very close, but after personal issues turned into quarrels, I had to remove her from my life for a period. My mother struggled with being a victim for many years. She had her own anger issues, so I had to remove her from my life. I had to have a hard conversation with one of my best friends as well and say, "You have too many problems surrounding your life. I cannot be your friend right now because I'm trying to change my life. I'm trying to turn some things around for my family."

My friend struggled to hear this. We'd been best friends since the sixth grade. It felt like a breakup. He called several times and said how much our friendship meant to him. And he wasn't angry, just sad. But he had so many things to work through, and at that time, he was pretty dependent on me and our friendship. I couldn't be depended on, and he needed to work through some tough things in his life by himself. I loved him enough to tell him this directly. When it came to other people, I needed to cut for various reasons, I just stopped taking their calls, or I would block their numbers.

I was going through my own tough spot. I didn't have time to deal with my friend's problems. He wasn't highlighting me for all the good I was doing in my life, for what I am capable of. He wasn't lifting me up.

In a twist, many people I removed from my life are now back.

I believe it's more caring to be honest with the people you do care deeply about.

They might be angry at first and won't want to accept your refusal to be in contact with them. They might accuse you of trying to be better than them when they see you changing your life. But they might also start accepting that their life isn't going so great and take the steps to fix it.

THE HARD CUTS THAT NEED TO HAPPEN

So many of those people, including my mother, my friend, and my sister, are all back in my life. We did separate for years because that's what I needed to do for myself.

> **If you are intent on rising through the levels, the more elite business owners and entrepreneurs who you want as a part of your network won't want to do business with you if you don't have your shit together.**

The quickest way to rise is to make the hard cuts now. Eliminate the people trying to put limitations on you, the people trying to drag you down, the people who are not there to support you. As you banish specific people, remember to also make the hard cuts on the environments that aren't good for you.

How to Walk Away

Pay attention to how you feel around certain people and places. Once you identify your feelings, take the steps to sever yourself. Execute a plan to remove these places and people. Don't go to the bar. If people invite you out to where you know you shouldn't be, stop taking their phone calls.

As you put your foot down, you'll notice patterns, like the days and times people call you when they want to drag you into these situations and places. Pay attention, and you'll know what times not to answer their phone calls. If you do have contact with them, then get good at saying no.

I'm a huge believer in being a yes man, but not in every option presented to me. I'm a yes man when it comes to opportunity and putting deals together. Saying yes has helped me achieve success. But to get there, I had to improve in saying no to a lot of people in my life. I had to smoothly refuse invitations to places that I didn't want to go to—that weren't going to serve me anymore. I had to stay strong to change my life.

As you level up your environment and the people around you, don't make it harder than it has to be. It will be difficult to follow through and implement your boundaries because of the emotion you've attached to specific people and places. Once you realize that, it should get a little easier to say no—because you can recognize *why* you feel a stronger connection. The good news is, the more you say no, the better you will get at it.

An old saying by someone whose name escapes me goes, "Only a habit can subdue another habit "The choice is yours, but obviously, a good habit replacing a bad one will be more productive.

If you feel overwhelmed about embarking on your plan, start taking steps in the right direction. After identifying who you want to be out of contact with, make choices to take fewer or no calls from them. Stop frequenting places where you shouldn't be going.

When you start spending time in different environments, you'll be amazed at how it leads to more positive environments. One great experience or opportunity will lead you to the next one—just like one shitty thing will lead you to another. If you're not sure what other environments to swap out for your current ones, go to the gym. Spend your free time at a community center, donate your time or even go to church. That worked for me.

CHAPTER 9

STEP IN A NEW DIRECTION

*"Sometimes, in the waves of change,
we find our true direction."*
—Unknown

When I was going through my divorce, my son, Kayden, came to me and said, "I want to get baptized." We weren't really a church-going family, but a lot of his friends were baptized, and he wasn't. He wanted to know what that was all about, so I said, "Okay, buddy, let's start going to church."

We went to church for a solid year while I was going through therapy. I wasn't dating during this time or even open to meeting new women. I was just working on myself—going to therapy every single week and attending different therapy groups—which also changed my environment. Making these adjustments in my life helped me work on my issues and become a better person for myself, my family, and my business.

I had started going to church for my son, and then I made the decision to start dating again. That's when all the women at church wanted to set me up with their nieces, daughters, friends' daughters, and so on.

I thought that was pretty cool. How else was I going to meet a quality woman? It wouldn't be through hanging out at the bar.

Also, in church, I heard about other activities and groups that were good for me. These were more positive steps in the right direction.

Try the Gym

As luck would have it, my next-door neighbor also went to the church we had decided to attend. Then he asked me to go to the gym with him. In my lifetime, I've been the king of the health yo-yo. I've been fit. I've been fat. I've been fit. I've been fat. I've been fit again. I now know that business is better when you're fit—it attracts more people to you.

I can't count how many of our employees and top leaders in our company I met through the gym. The best leaders within our organization today are people who go to the gym daily. They constantly work on their health.

Like attracts like, and don't forget in a world where you can't control much, you can control that.

You can take steps to start controlling your environment. Those little steps make one little shift, which makes a huge difference in the trajectory of your business. Sometimes, you won't realize the path you're forging for yourself until years later.

That's what I'm going through right now.

As I'm writing this book, I realize all the people who not only came from the gym but who came from the people I met at the gym—who are a positive part of our environment now.

Business Masterminds and Groups

Another step I took to improve my life was getting involved in business masterminds and groups. When you engage in these areas, you'll attend conferences for your industry. You'll meet the people seeking growth in their lives and business. Just like you, they will be fully open to meeting more people—and they will also be working on improving their lives.

> **Since you will have made the hard cuts of certain people, habits, and places, you'll have a lot more room for the right kind of people in your life.**

They will turn into referral partners and people who will recommend you. These people will possibly want to work for you, but it all starts with taking those initial steps.

While I had a lot of experience in achieving personal growth through my years of therapy, there was something special and different about going to business events, masterminds, and groups. Developing my network through these groups led my partners and me down a path of growing in all aspects of our life, not just our business. When I learned from people who operated at higher levels than me, I took what they taught me and shared it with our company.

Sharing improved the company's visions and goals, enabling the other leaders and me to share our newfound knowledge with our sales, fulfillment, and customer service teams. We inspired people because we were inspired.

Buddy

Any doubts we had about our recent positive influences disappeared when one of our longstanding employees, Buddy, was offered a position at a different company. This new place promised him a percentage of ownership. As he weighed his decision, I remember him pulling Trevor and me aside and saying, "I've got this opportunity I don't think I can pass up."

After he explained his situation to us, I stressed: "Make sure you get the agreement in writing. We're not here to hold you back. It might be the greatest opportunity for you; it might not be. Either way, it'll work out. It'll be a learning lesson, or it won't, but we wish you the best of luck.

We truly just want success for you. You've been a great asset to us. While we hate to see you go, we want you to keep winning, brother."

Buddy thanked us and went on his way, although leaving was very hard for him. He brought a ton of value to that other company. But after seven months, the new company didn't follow through on certain promises to him. They also didn't have a culture of winning or growth. That mattered to Buddy.

That's when he called us up and said, "I know that I've probably burned this bridge, or maybe you don't have room for me … but if you do, I'd love an opportunity to come back."

Because Buddy was an asset, we said, "You're the one guy we could make some room for." Even though we weren't really hiring at that time, we welcomed him back. By then, we'd replaced Buddy with another person intent on working in a culture of winning. They were both quality people, so we made allowances to keep them on. When new people come on board, they quickly get on our trajectory. They buy into our culture and environment.

Why?

Because our company is a positive and authentic place—precisely why Buddy wanted to come back to it.

As Buddy and the rest of the team and I discussed his return, he clarified, "Yes, I made more money with you guys, but that's not the reason I want to come back. I've missed being around people who want to continue to grow, people who want to push each other."

If we had not made those hard cuts in our business, we wouldn't have had a healthy environment and culture. That is the value of environment.

Pay attention to what you are creating in your life, and consider, too, if you've plateaued—as everyone has at some points in their lives—certain elements in your environment probably aren't that positive.

What Your Life Looks Like is up to You

If you want to facilitate a winning environment in your business, you must take the necessary steps to get there. Understand that you are the reflection and pulse of your business. If you walk into the office every day and spread around the energy of a poo cloud, it's because you're a poo cloud. You're the influence people attach to.

Take responsibility for what you bring into the room. Whether you're the owner of the company or trying to quit your job and start your own company, you have to make room in your life to allow the right people to come in. Then you will not only begin to succeed in your business and life, but you can also use your positive influence to push your business, family, and anyone else in your life to new levels.

Social Media Sets Your Mindset

When I turn on my social media and scroll through the newsfeeds, I don't see any negativity. All the people I've met over the last ten years have replaced the people I've cut out of my life who haven't served me, who haven't highlighted me, and who haven't lifted me up.

But I do want to stress that people aren't replaceable. I went through the agony of walking away from people who made up large portions of my life, and it was hard and hurt. I had to work through it. You can learn to love people from a distance if they are not in your life—and of course, wish them well.

There will be the rare occasion when I do feel low and in a rut, but because I'm constantly surrounded by positivity and growth, I can come out of my rut much quicker. Instead of sinking into the despair of the acts of the people facing deep life struggles, the people I'm surrounded with are pushing themselves. When I witness this, I can see more clearly what needs work in my life. I can see the excuses that are keeping me where I am. I can pull myself up and say, "This is bullshit. If they're pushing through, I can push through, as well. I don't have the patience or time for excuses."

If we're going to go from good to great, we must do what's not easy.

When I look back at what we've done in the last ten years in our business, it's incredible. I know the biggest factor has been the choices our leaders made to level up their environments and networks.

CHAPTER 10

PRE-JUDGMENT IS A COST!

"Judgment will only serve you after the intentions of the one you judge are known."
—Kale Goodman

As I type out the first paragraph of this chapter, I want to acknowledge that it would be hypocritical to say I've been particularly good at not judging people. That's just not true.

We're all human. We do judge, and we do judge a lot.

We also pay a costly price in business—especially when it comes to networking—when we pre-judge people based on appearances or differences before we even get to know them.

I've had to become more self-aware of my tendency to do this. I've had to shift my pre-judgments because of particular events in my life.

Shifting my pre-judgments has allowed me to open more doors. It's allowed more people into my network.

If we want more results from our network, we need to have more options. So, why limit our options by pre-judging people before we even have the opportunity to know them and what they're capable of? Before we can determine what their strengths and weaknesses are, what their business is, and if they align with what we need or want in our business, we shut any opportunity with them down, and that's not right… or smart.

Stopping Pre-Judgment

Setting aside my pre-judgments has served me in my network. A couple of experiences jump to my mind that I will share with you.

Even though I did pre-judge certain people, especially in these scenarios, I was able and willing to set my pre-judgments aside to get to know people at a deeper level.

Right Out of the Gate

I remember my first sales job. As I mentioned, it was a different culture. A lot of people, including me, were learning the ropes. I was there to make more money, so I listened to a lot of people and, unfortunately, heard their pre-judgments about the leads we were to call.

Certain salespeople did not want to talk to prospects based on what they did for a living, their ethnicity, the part of the country they lived in, etc. They figured, assumed, and pre-judged that specific people would be broke.

Salespeople were trained to get off the phone quickly if they discovered an engineer was on the other end. Engineers were known to over-analyze and pick everything apart. They asked a lot of questions—which certain salespeople equated to wasting their time. The assumption was that engineers were not going to buy our product or service because they had a lot to consider before they'd actually buy. The same "logic" applied to doctors.

Sadly, some short-sighted salespeople regarded certain ethnic groups in the same manner. Some people wouldn't want to talk to black people because they were afraid that they would take a lot of their time and act as if they had the capability to join the program, but that they couldn't come up with the money—especially if they lived in a certain part of the world.

They might regard a black man living in a rougher inner city as taking their time and being unable to buy. I saw them treat Asian folks in California as if they would also take a lot of their time and not buy on the spot. They snubbed white people in certain parts of the country. A white person in New Mexico, for example, was assumed to have no money and live in a trailer park.

These pre-judgments limited leads for the stereotyping salespeople. As a new guy in sales, I overheard these pre-judgments and knew I had to make a choice. I would ask myself: *are you not going to call certain leads based on their name and state like some of these salespeople?* Or *are you going to call the leads to get to know people at a deeper level?*

In those moments before I called the leads, sure, the pre-judgment flashed across my mind, but I shoved it away. I was resolved to be a hard worker and reject those pre-judgments, so I'd still call the lead and learn about the person.

I was new to the sales team and thought I might as well be doing the work anyway. Why would I call fewer leads when I had the same number of hours in a day as anyone else? I didn't want to leave any potential commission on the table.

But I noticed that as I continued to grow and close more sales than other reps, it was because I called more people.

**I dialed the people they didn't want to—
those they assumed would not be worth their time.**

I would call the engineers and spend more time with them—because that's all they wanted. I would talk to the doctors about the marketing problems they were having in their company. All they needed was to gather information and or someone to get to know them a little better—that allowed me to set them up for a sale later.

When I came across names that some of the other salespeople wouldn't call, I would call them. You'd be surprised how many times people wouldn't call someone by the name of Muhammad because they assumed he was a new immigrant without an established credit score or that he'd be in a financial situation preventing him from buying our product. After calling Muhammad, I would learn he had been born and raised in America and that he was perfectly capable of coming up with the dollars needed to buy our product.

Yes, I called all the damn leads. It was in my best interest to do so, despite their name, location, or profession.

As I became a top salesman, I had pointed discussions with those reps shutting out certain prospects.

With my numbers dominating the board, everyone wanted to know, "What are you doing differently?" "How come your close ratio is higher than mine?" "Are you getting more leads than me?"

Without knowing what I had promised myself I would do, they figured the boss was giving me more leads. That's half the truth for the super closers, but it wasn't my case. If you have better numbers, you do get more leads—and you should—since you are trying to create leads for the company as you are selling. But I wasn't there yet.

In having the conversations with people in the sales group who wanted to know my secret, I told them: "I just call all the leads, man. I'm not going to refuse to call someone because they're black, Asian, it's assumed they live in a trailer park, or they're an engineer and supposed to be a waste of time." As I sat on the edge of my desk, I explained my tactics to my curious audience, finishing with: "I sold an engineer last week."

Refusing to go down the road of pre-judgment also served me well in door-to-door sales. My aim, again, was to make more money.

PRE-JUDGMENT IS A COST!

During the time when I was selling solar in California and running a business on the side, I found myself in a rough patch of San Diego. The rumor was that these neighborhoods were known to be a waste of time.

Of course, the owner of the solar company told me to knock the highest caliber, gated neighborhoods. "Go knock those doors," he said. Well, I tried, but it was tough. I couldn't get anybody to talk to me. In the middle of the day, most people weren't home. The high achievers in those neighborhoods were out, so I didn't have a lot of luck.

I had the same results with the upper-middle-class. Even the lower-middle-class, where people worked longer hours, keeping them away from home more, didn't produce as well as some of the poorer neighborhoods.

Selling there helped me in another way, too. When I started, I was a little rusty—as all beginners are. I just needed people to hear my sales pitch, so I could get better at my presentation.

Again, I went against the grain. While everyone told me not to knock certain neighborhoods, I thought, *I don't care what neighborhoods I work. Lemme knock these doors.*

It paid off. I met people, and they heard my script—which led to me improving.

I did have to filter through people who didn't have the money or credit to qualify for the product. But a lot more people could listen to me in live mode. Everybody knows that pitching someone in person is a lot different than pitching somebody in your imagination.

So, I knocked the doors based on the neighborhood I was in, which allowed me to get better at the sales pitch, which allowed me to close more deals.

I closed more deals in the poorer neighborhoods than anybody else on our team. But I also closed more deals than anyone else in the middle-class and higher-end neighborhoods—all because I set aside the pre-judgments of certain neighborhoods.

People are people. Until you open up to them and allow them to open up to you, you won't know what their credit score is. You won't know what problems you could potentially solve with your product or service.

I observed what worked and what didn't with people as time went on. I didn't choose to talk to people because I knew it would work. I only did what I was tasked with doing—and through that, I learned how to dominate the board.

In working my areas, I figured out quickly that pre-judgments aren't true.

If I had listened to the other reps' pre-judgments, I wouldn't have gotten the reps in that I needed to get better at my craft. I wouldn't have found the deals I did, which gave me the confidence to get into other neighborhoods.

Haru

Haru was an old friend of mine and an interesting fellow. I met him at a Halloween party at my home in 2007.

We had started. The company in 2006, and around 2007, we were still trying to gain meaningful momentum. So, I threw a Halloween party. Some college kids were invited, and they brought some friends.

In this mix of kids was Haru. When I met him, he was a lingerer, but he was different. Instantly, I knew he had a unique personality.

PRE-JUDGMENT IS A COST!

But a lot of people didn't take the time to get to know Haru. As he tried to get close with people, they would brush him off. He struggled because he wasn't a great people person. For some reason, Haru gravitated to me, and I don't dismiss people. But I will admit, I did pre-judge Haru. I wasn't going to completely shut him out or be disrespectful to him. That's not who I am. So, I allowed Haru to enter my life.

Because I opened my life to Haru, he became a friend. Although, I do remember many moments of frustrations with Haru, even to the point where I sometimes didn't want to and wouldn't take his call. If he did show up on a few occasions, I didn't want to give him the time of day. But I did because I didn't have it in my heart to be rude to him.

Haru wanted to work for me, which he did. And because Haru was unique, he wasn't that proficient in sales. But that's what we were hiring for—we wanted a great rep on the phone. As time went on, Haru didn't work out. I told him: "Right now, I just can't put the leads in your hands. You're not converting. I'm so sorry, dude. You need to find something else to do. You can't work here anymore."

With no hard feelings, Haru went on to develop software that was used for selling training in the foreign exchange market. Our company was trying to teach people how to make money in that market, and we had developed a great course that produced high success rates. While Haru couldn't sell that product, he went to many conferences to promote his software and did secure results for certain clients. Over time, he earned a little momentum with his software. Even though Haru couldn't work with us, I always hoped he would do great. As he developed his product, he would periodically check in with me. Haru is an example of working in your strengths and finding what you're skilled in. The kid was relentless.

One quality I admired in Haru was that he could approach anybody. He didn't have a fear of rejection—even though he had been discounted by so many people. I thought that was awesome.

Over the years, my love for Haru grew. I loved him for who he was, but had I not gotten to know him at a deeper level like other people, I would have pre-judged him, assumed that he was annoying, and couldn't bring any value to me. I probably wouldn't have stayed connected to him.

Because I had a big heart for Haru, I got to know him a little more and gave him a chance to work at our company. Although it didn't work out, he was so grateful that I even took a shot on him—so he always wanted to stay in my life. Come to find out, that Haru had all these strengths most people didn't know about. He knew how to build trading software. He went to events and promoted his product and himself. Upon his return, he always brought people to me that we could help. Since I had chosen to care about him, Haru talked highly of me to others.

"You've got to meet my buddy, Kale," Haru would say. "He's a great business owner with an insane skill for making money."

Haru piqued people's interest to get on the phone with me. These people also had courses in the foreign exchange market or had some sort of connection to the industry; sometimes, they even had their own brokerages. Haru introducing people to me created valuable conversations. I met some fascinating people through his willingness to approach others and keep trying to push through, even though he had faced so many people walking away from him in his life. To this day, I still have people in my network because of him.

One referral led to another to another. While I'm not in the business of the foreign exchange market anymore, I met clever people who knew online marketing, how to write software, and who knew of data connections to other people who were also great at creating data. This new network all stemmed from Haru making a few introductions to me.

The crazy thing about Haru is that he disappeared one day. Search and rescue went out looking for him. They found his wrecked car in a ditch in the middle of Arizona.

Even today, nobody knows what happened to Haru. He was never found.

I've thought a lot about Haru. He was supposed to be at my wedding a couple of months after he went missing. When he didn't show up, I knew something was wrong. When he stopped replying to all my messages, a pit of fear grew in my stomach. He wouldn't have skipped out on our wedding. He was ecstatic to be a part of it.

Haru didn't have many meaningful friendships. But he evolved into a great friend in my family. My kids loved him. My wife loved him. My dog loved him. He was a genuinely good person.

I'll never forget that I would never have gotten to know Haru if I had done what most people did to him—if I had pre-judged him so much that he would have never been known by me. Haru was an interesting character that, for some reason, people dismissed often.

Our relationship allowed me to find out about all his other wonderful traits. Haru brought great value to my life.

Pre-Judging has Nothing to Do with Safety

Sometimes it serves people well to be aware and on alert. That's not pre-judgment. I'm talking about assuming the worst of someone when your personal safety is not a factor. Do this wrong, and there's a huge cost to everyone involved, especially if you do it often and incorrectly.

Let people into your life. Give them the extra time to get to know them more and find out if they do align somewhere in your life. Setting aside pre-judgment has become an increasing goal of mine over the years, learned through my real-life experiences.

More doors are opened by judging people based on their actions as an individual versus a group they're tied to.

I'm super, super grateful to have discovered where pre-judgment costs most people and how I can use that to my advantage. I challenge you to spend some time thinking about your own pre-judgment habits.

Are you willing to be honest with yourself about where you pre-judge?

Are you willing to work against your pre-judgment and have more conversations with the people you typically wouldn't talk to?

Can you set your pre-judgments aside to get to know people more, to find out where you can give to them and where they can give to you?

Chapter 11

GREED KILLS

Greed is a bottomless pit which exhausts the person in an endless effort to satisfy the need without ever reaching satisfaction.
—Erich Fromm

Before I started my first business, I had the privilege of working for an accounting firm in a sales role. This was a pivotal opportunity in becoming a business owner. I'm forever grateful for my time at this firm. It was awesome, especially in the beginning.

I believed in this product for multiple reasons. One, because I grew up in a home that had a ton of tax troubles, and two, working at an accounting firm helped solve a lot of those issues.

I was also super fortunate to learn several things from the owner of that tax and accounting company. He was a great mentor of mine with a strong personality. He was a huge risk-taker and a person who carried himself with a lot of confidence. I was drawn to him.

Most people feared him because he was direct. I could see that he was extremely passionate. He would rip into your ass if you didn't do things his way. So, I learned what to do and what not to do, which is a superpower. If you can learn from other people, you'll win the game a lot quicker than if you must figure out everything on your own.

In my time at this company, I paid attention to how he operated, how he approached people, how he brought business in, how he ran his company, and how he handled his managers and departments. He allowed me to get a little bit closer to him, which was awesome because I just wanted to learn as much as I could from him. Now, he was a busy guy and in and out of the office a lot, but when he was in town, I was one of the lucky ones who went to lunch with him. In return, he respected me because I worked hard and was a top sales representative.

> **When he decided to take his company to the next level, it was a big risk. He opened an office in downtown Manhattan, New York City, the financial mecca of the world.**

His goal was to improve the perception of his company and take it to the next level with strong, healthy numbers.

I was super honored when he told me he wanted me to go out to New York City for a week and work with some of his new sales representatives on opening the new office.

One of my co-workers and I traveled out there and spent some time with the new office's team. It didn't take us long to figure out that these guys didn't need any help from us. So, we started mentoring them and showing them how we ran our Utah office.

This new sales team had a different energy; they were next-level hustlers. When they were on calls, they used words we didn't. They had different rebuttals and different strategies. What they did, worked very quickly. There's just something about the New York hustler versus the relaxed West Utah hustler. People on the East Coast have a different edge than the salespeople I've grown up around. The new team epitomized go, go, go.

When I came home, I felt a bit insecure. *Man, I could do a lot more. These guys are already putting up numbers that we've reached, and they're brand new*—they haven't been doing it near as long as we have—was all I could think.

The people in this new office had a totally different drive. Observing this about them helped me step up my game. Fast-forward about a year into the New York office's existence. Their sales guys were not only doing more numbers than us; before long, their sales streak passed us. Then their team expanded beyond our team's size.

> **That was the beginning of an end for me.**

I had been so inspired by working with my boss and becoming a top representative in a tax and accounting company that it gave me the confidence to start a side hustle. I saw that the other office was doing so much more than us and that I needed to have something lined up for me if the company moved its operations to New York City. I couldn't relocate there. My home, family, and life were in Utah.

Shortly after I launched my company, my boss pulled me into his office and said, "This is a hard conversation. You've contributed a lot to the company, but I'm kicking you off the fence. I heard you're moonlighting, and I can tell your focus here has changed…."

Now I was puzzled because my performance hadn't really slipped. I replied, "I'm not disagreeing with you, but I'm still the number two guy."

As I'd flung open the doors to my business, I'd slipped from the number one sales guy to number two. I also pointed out that some of these other guys at the bottom of the totem pole weren't doing even near the numbers I was.

My boss held up his hand and said, "It's not about the numbers. I just can't employ people who have another business on the side. I need people here who are fully bought into what I'm doing."

He was right, but I wasn't happy about it. It wasn't the optimal way to end my employment. He smiled for a second, then said with a wave of his hand, which I took to mean I should get up and walk out, "At the end of the day, you'll probably thank me, but for now, you're done."

True to his word, he fired me.

What Now?

I didn't know it yet, but I was about to enter a super hard time of my life. Even though I did have a side hustle with my partner, Jeremy, and I loved what we were doing after hours, I was forced to go all-in—although, after just a year running the new business, I wasn't ready.

While I had no intention of competing with my old boss, I did take a lot of what I learned from him and channeled it into my company. In addition, I partnered with more accountants and partners to fully develop our company. It was a lot of work.

Then, I was in for a surprise. As we grew in relevance, my old boss slapped me with a lawsuit.

When I was served, I called him in an uncontrollable fury. "What are you doing? Why would you sue me over this? My intention is not to go after any of your employees or business relationships. I'm not trying to take your referral partners. I'm not even trying to run my business like yours."

My old boss definitely had a big ego, and he was about to let me see it.

After I was done protesting, he said with a shrug in his voice, "I don't really care. I don't feel good about what you're doing. The bottom line is that you're just getting started and already stepping on my turf. Kale, it doesn't matter to me if I win this lawsuit or not. I'll spend a couple hundred thousand just to make sure that I put you out of business. I've got the funds to lose, and you don't."

> **My brain screamed:** *you're suing me to put me out of business? Who do you think you are?*

Greed doesn't serve people well. Neither does paranoia, and I was on the receiving end of it. He did exactly what he said he was going to do, spent several hundred thousand dollars trying to put us out of business. While it was tough for us, we were able to pull from our other businesses and survive. The foothold we had gained in our tax and accounting business gave us the ability to outlast his threats. In the end, we didn't spend near as much money as he did, but we won our case.

> **Winning our case allowed us to remain in business.**

I'm sure my old boss felt the sting of us winning. Because of his greed, he spent a lot of money to try and put us out of business just to prove a point—and he failed.

When the "Mighty" Fall

After another year or two, our business grew to about eight figures, fueled by our book of business, referral partners, and the new onboarding sales we were going to make. Still, we weren't doing near the numbers our old boss was doing. He had scaled his company to what I heard was a nine-figure company doing over $100 million a year in business.

I couldn't figure out how he'd done that in such a short time span. Even though the New York office brought a crazy different energy, the explosion of growth that happened after I exited his company didn't make sense.

Then I heard in the news that his company was caught up in a sales practices investigation. That confused me because when I worked for him, I remembered not being allowed to veer from scripts, mark sales above the package prices, or say anything high-pressure or misleading. We were monitored heavily and had to follow a certain protocol and go through the proper compliance channels to ensure every deal was ethical and clean. I suspect as my greedy ex-boss' NYC office grew, his newly hired COO turned a blind eye in favor of all the money they were making. This company morphed into a massive powerhouse only to be shut down by certain regulatory agencies in New York.

My old boss bought private jets and multiple homes all over the nation. Then he got himself into a spot where he couldn't afford his numbers to ever dip. The partners he had brought in for the New York office had reduced their practices to center around only grabbing cash while providing no value. It was completely unethical. Just sell, sell, sell, grab cash, and get as much as you can out of every customer.

It must've been like trying to turn off a fully opened faucet. He was a great entrepreneur and had built an amazing company, but as it continued to grow and the wrong people came in, his greed and those wrong people brought out the worst of his intentions. Materialism got the best of him. Right before the investigation, he sold off his shares to the COO in the New York office because (I think) he saw the writing on the wall.

I've been in the game now for 17 years and have seen a lot of companies follow a similar pattern. They get away from their original core beliefs. They get away from the integrity they based their business on—because of the new levels they've created that provide a more elite lifestyle, which poses certain challenges. It takes a great deal of willingness to stop that.

Can you imagine having to shut down a nine-figure company because you don't believe in it anymore? Even if you didn't have to shut the company down and had to make some decisions that would cut the numbers in half or more, most people could do that, but they wouldn't because of what the business provided. They couldn't give up the lifestyle.

> **I can't say that if I hadn't learned from seeing it with my own two eyes that I wouldn't have gone down that same path.**

But because of this experience, I'm determined to make sure that we follow our core values and don't let greed get the best of us. That we don't let it put us in a similar situation as we are desperate to grow. Knowing what I do now, I am much more willing to expand at a slower pace to make sure we're doing everything right. Moving too fast could put us out of business if we do it for the wrong reason.

There are so many areas in which greed can kill your deals, especially in a business like mine, where we depend on referral partners and people wanting to do business with us.

We must make decisions that aren't going to affect our referral partners' businesses negatively. We must put together deals that will only affect their business positively if we want our relationship to last over the long haul.

CHAPTER 12

HOW TO AVOID BEING GREEDY IN BUSINESS

"Greed is a bottomless pit, which exhausts the person in an endless effort to satisfy the need without ever reaching satisfaction."
—Erich Fromm

If you apply the following tips to your business, you can avoid making the following mistakes that many people on a similar journey as you have made.

Cash Grabbing vs. Investing Extra into Your Customers

1. **Care:** If you care more about getting revenue from sales and fulfilling orders as cheaply as possible, you are delivering crap instead of value.

   Not only will this bite you in the long run due to chargebacks and cancels but you will end up spending time and money solving those problems. It pays off to invest the extra cost to deliver the goods above board. Cash grabbing will also kill the trust in your referral network. People feel it when you half-ass. If you're always trying to increase your bottom line by servicing the customer less, they will feel scorned. When they are scorned, it gets back to the referral source. The last thing you want is a referral partner losing faith in your service.

   Put money first, and you will also kill the opportunity of turning your customers into your referral sources. If you feel taken advantage of by a company, are you going to refer your friends to them? Of course, not. But you'd be surprised how much that happens ... all to keep up with a lifestyle.

2. **Hanging up on Negotiations:** When it comes to making referral deals in the business-to-business world, don't fixate on getting the most or winning. Transparency is key. Most deals work out for a longer period when there's openness about what you can and can't do.

Lying or undercutting when you are negotiating is a greed move. Just as your customers will know your true intentions, so, too, will your affiliates or referral partners.

Stingy behavior creates the opposite of loyalty, which means your competition can slip in and snatch up your clients much more easily.

When I am ready to sit down and negotiate, I think, *I am a yes man!* I refuse to lose out on an opportunity over a few percentage points. As long as I can make it work, I say yes! I don't look at deals short-term, but I seek the value over the course of the relationship. If I'm cutting the numbers close, I remember that I have an opportunity to show the affiliate what we're capable of.

Once our arrangement is dialed in and we're firing on all cylinders, I can always go back to the table with data and ammo to reconfigure our agreement so it works for both parties. If you've done a great job and you're transparent on why it makes more sense to meet in the middle, the renegotiation almost always happens. On these terms, you don't need to worry about losing a relationship. By this time, the other party should see the value.

You're not trying to create a win-win situation. You're striving to create a triple-win situation. Of course, you and your partner need to come to terms, but the most important person who needs to win is the customer.

I've seen the customer repeatedly lose in these negotiations. When you and your partner can't agree on certain percentages or numbers, the compromise centers on the customer—who suffers raised prices. That's another form of greed kicking in!

Don't do that to your customers, please.

Raising your prices is sometimes necessary. But not when the only justification for doing so is to satisfy your referral sources.

In the thick of negotiations, I have told the affiliate the following to get them to see reason. I lock eyes with them and say, "I'd hate to have to charge your customer more than market value to make a deal work. We really want to provide the best experience to your client, so you look great for referring them, they get great service, and we get a new customer. That's a triple win."

Good business people will see the value in that plan. Yes, businesses monetize and refer customers for money, but if they care about their brand, they will want to make a little less to ensure their customer has a wonderful experience.

How you negotiate referral costs and what you charge to your customers is a great way to gauge your greed factor.

If you're okay saying, "I'll just charge your customer more" or "I'll just cut this value out of the deal," etc., what you're saying is, "I don't care about your customer. I only want their money." Most great businesses and brands don't respect that. I've also found that when I've made deals with folks who care more about the money versus the customer that it hasn't served me well.

If that's their mindset, they typically haven't taken care of their customer. Then regardless of how great you do, you can get lumped into customer complaints—because of their bad behavior. It really does go both ways.

Small business owners have reported us to the BBB (Better Business Bureau) in their dispute, but they only named us because the company that referred them to us did them wrong. These customers who suffered at the hands of the unscrupulous company and who wanted their money back assumed we were a bad business, as well. It's guilt by association—so be careful who you align with and make sure your values match.

Don't be greedy. It won't serve you long-term. And don't take business from greedy people because if they're not interested in the triple win, they will drag down your brand with them.

3. **Create a Set of Standards and Stick to Them**: You will be tested in this area when you're in the referral game, and it's harder to maintain your standards than you might think.

   Yes, you want to make deals. Yes, you're in business for the money, and yes, you're interested in getting the most out of your life. But acting out of greed won't get you the most out of *your* life. Greed kills your business's longevity, and it can cause a reset in your business. If you reach this point, it's only a matter of time before wanting too much catches up with you and forces you to go out of business or start over.

   If it sounds like I'm speaking from experience, I am. When I wanted the numbers and the quick results, I didn't have the wisdom to get out of my current mindset and think ahead into the future.

   As the old saying goes: "Pigs get fat, but hogs get slaughtered." I'm sure you can think of some stories where greed has led to folks getting slaughtered in their business.

HOW TO AVOID BEING GREEDY IN BUSINESS

When you are tempted to ask for too much or are fixated on the wrong goal, remember that greed will kill many things in your business, but what it mostly kills is your deals.

To recap....

- Don't be a greedy deal maker.

- Don't do deals with greedy deal makers.

- Your referral partners will spot greed in you if you don't care about the customer.

- You can spot greed in your referral partners when they don't care about their customers.

- Look for the triple-win deals, not just the double wins.

- Greed will ruin the longevity of your brand.

- Are you willing to give a little to make sure you create a triple win?

Are you willing to step up, show your value and renegotiate later to make the deal happen?

Are you willing to turn business away for the longevity of your company, to preserve your name as a quality business or networker when you spot greed on the other side of the deal?

CHAPTER 13

BUILDING AND EVALUATING YOUR BUSINESS

"Efficiency is doing better what is already being done. Effectiveness is deciding what to do better"
—Peter F. Drucker

The idea of building an awesome life is to live it.

Don't forget that!

At some point, as you are running your business, you should seek to replace yourself. That's the whole point of living that awesome life you dream of!

There are levels to getting to that point, it takes time, and you can't do it alone. But you can do it.

In almost all cases, if you build a business alone, just know that most businesses are not worth much.

Why?

Because you're selling a job, and most people are not looking to buy a job.

Measuring Your Business' Value

Let's assume you own a landscaping maintenance company. You have no employees or team and hardly any systems or processes. Then the time comes to sell the business and retire. Can you picture the person who might want to buy your business? That market is very small.

I picture a person in their 20s to 30s working a job for $40,000 a year who would love to make $80,000-100,000. But there are some problems with this scenario. First, the business won't be worth that much money to allow the potential buyer to make what they want. Second, a person with that kind of work history could only come up with so much money.

First, they likely can't come up with the money, and even if they could, your business is worth your equipment and customer base. That's about it—which means your buyer is already uninterested.

There must be an upside to the buyer.
They have to see how they can get ahead to make a profit.

That's going to take some time since your business revolves around serving your customer base.

Clearly, this new owner would need to make enough profit to cover their operating costs and lifestyle in purchasing a business like that. More importantly, to justify the deal, there would need to be enough upside.

Maybe a business like this would sell for $50,000-60,000 because the only value is the equipment and customer base.

There's nothing wrong with that.

Those types of businesses sell all the time. Hopefully, the people who buy that company would love cutting grass and would be filled with joy at owning your business.

My point is that a high revenue and profiting business that has teams, systems, processes, branding, and a reputation is going to sell for far more. It would be a turnkey business with leadership and management in place so the new owner wouldn't have to take on much at all. That's a far cry from our first scenario.

Let's say it's another landscape company for sale has 50 crews servicing thousands of yards in the wealthiest neighborhoods. They've instituted technology to track their teams and production. They have loyal customers, and their numbers are tracked to a tee.

In this case, you would attract all kinds of potential buyers. If the numbers make sense, a buyer will offer three to five times the annual profit. This means if the company is making a profit of $2 million a year, it could be worth $10 million to a new buyer of that business, knowing they will come out ahead on that business year after year with positive cash flow.

After comparing these two situations, think about what you would want if you were buying a business. Chances are, you would only be interested in buying a business with the highest likelihood of making more money to secure your future. You will not want a business that will end up owning you.

In building your business, that's exactly where your mind should be. Aim to answer this question: *how can I build my business to be so turnkey that many people would desire to buy it?* An investment that makes sense to others is a business with value that allows the purchaser to go liquid if they ever did need or want to.

Maybe your goal is to never sell. Maybe you want to hand down your business to your children. Regardless of your plans, build it to be worth something with the aim that anyone would want it.

Building smart also means you have the freedom of knowing you can leave with your family on vacations and that nothing will implode while you're gone. You can go on with business as usual when an employee takes a vacation or is sick since you have the right teams to get the job done.

That is one of the major reasons I wanted to be a business owner. Freedom of my time is an ultimate motivator for me and almost every other business owner.

As you get your feet under you, you won't get to that stage right away. You will need to take multiple steps to cross that finish line. But again (and I will keep saying this), you can get there.

When your doors first open, you will wear all the hats. That's okay and normal. I am going to give you some ideas to think about that will shortcut your startup pain as you build your business.

Phases of Building Your Business

Employee Mindset

As you know, I started as a sales guy. Yep, even a "sales guy" can build systems, processes, and teams. I couldn't doubt myself. I had to possess an empowered mindset to get to the next phase.

Today, I'm extremely grateful for my background in sales. Take a page out of my book and feel confident that you can benefit from your sales experience, too. If you are coming from a sales role and want to build a business, or if you're a hustler who loves money and who jumped into sales for a better life, you can relate to what I am saying.

For so many years, I was the guy who wanted two things: a phone and my leads—so I could make sales and a paycheck.

I did not want to think about the fulfillment process after the sale was made. I just wanted to get on to the next one to make the biggest check possible each week.

BUILDING AND EVALUATING YOUR BUSINESS

Self-Employed

In this stage, you're now responsible for much more than just yourself. You'll deal with building more than sales; you'll also have to make sure your customer gets the product or service they paid for.

You can't pass the buck after the sale. Besides, if your customer cancels, it comes right off your bottom line. That doesn't make much sense.

When you're self-employed, you're responsible for the sales, product or service development and delivery, and for the customer service. You're even the accountant knowing and growing the numbers.

As your baby grows, you have no choice but to bring people in to help you, and that means you're also the manager of people. You need leaders to step up and lighten your load so you can work more on the business rather than in the business. But … if you're like most people, you'll struggle with letting go. You'll get caught up in wanting it done your way, and you won't trust in others easily to do it the right way or your way. If you're battling this emotion, trust me, it's very common. The best choice you can make is to allow your team to make mistakes and learn. You must be there to guide them for a while. There is no way around it. You must go through this process for the long-term gain.

CEO—a Delegator

In this role, you can rise from a 1,000-foot view and see your business from a different perspective. You can identify needs, roles, leaders, and more. To go beyond this role and start tasting freedom, you must breed leaders in your organization.

Typically, a CEO is more of a visionary. To scale, they will often need a "side by side" leader. This leader should have different strengths, including operational skills, so the CEO can focus on their job without worrying about the business functions—which will all be funneled toward the COO. As a CEO, networking and cultivating the company's most valuable relationships and creating more connections from a growing network is crucial. If you are in this role, this is where you need to put your attention.

To be a next-level CEO and networker, you must be able to direct traffic as simply as possible.

An effective CEO has teams, systems, and processes in place that allow him or her to direct traffic to very few but effective places.

When you are moving from an employee to the self-employed mindset and then the employer mindset, you're directing traffic in 100 different ways.

You're not just handling sales. You're writing scripts and the training and marketing to create leads. You're hustling to get referrals, talking to customers after the sale to identify problems and fix them. You're hiring, firing, managing customer service, HR, and accounting all in one.

No matter who you are, when this is your routine, it will exhaust you, burn you out and make you feel like you're going crazy.

Picture yourself as the only traffic officer trying to direct every vehicle in Times Square or a congested London roundabout. I can't even imagine driving there, let alone directing traffic, but that's what you're doing when you're wearing all the hats in the early stages. You're directing a bunch of maniacs and will turn yourself into one, too.

Growing a business without defined roles, systems, processes, and solid checklists is like trying to be that solo traffic director. That's why I made it a part of my strategy to bring someone in as my partner to fulfill that

COO role of our multiple businesses. I wasn't the greatest at implementing systems or holding people accountable for each of their roles. I made a lot of money wearing multiple hats and directing that traffic, but I was capped out. So, I extended a partnership opportunity to Trevor. Not only is Trevor phenomenal in his role, but he has a strong gift of gab.

I was drawn to him as a partner because he was a natural leader. I needed that for our company mission to evolve. Other partners played key roles, but Trevor and I can produce business like no other.

The challenge in the early days of bringing Trevor on as a partner was that he didn't know his role either. No one had defined roles back then. I could see that he was talented in managing the sales teams, and I was skilled in managing business relationships.

Chapter 14

ELEVATING YOUR BUSINESS

*"You will either step forward into growth,
or you will step back into safety."*
—Abraham Maslow

We addressed the following four key elements to elevate our business to a new level, which created more revenue, profit, and freedom for both of us and our team.

1. **Undergo an Audit:** To gain needed perspective, we brought in outside eyeballs to check out our business. This team asked us to conduct a time audit of each partner, which was insanely valuable.

   We get so caught up in the day-to-day busy work that we don't stop to identify potential problems like where our time is going. What better way to do that than to conduct a self-audit? This audit uncovered many areas we needed to address and strengthen.

   With the truth of our business laid out, we could not only plug the holes, but we could create more roles and put people in the right spots. This audit also permitted us as owners and operators to see where we could delegate more to create more time for the most valuable areas of our business.

   It's hard to recognize the truth of a situation when you're in the trenches all the time. You might not even hear about some of the critical issues that affect your customer the most. These might not be complicated issues but could be as simple as no one answering or returning a client's call.

We learned about this problem affecting our business after the audit and had to work hard to fix it. Customers had been sending us emails from the Contact Us page on our site. They would say, "Why can't I get a hold of anyone? No one is calling me back." Then something worse happened.

More than once, our referral partners emailed and called us, saying pointedly: "My customer asked me what was going on over there. She said no one is answering or calling her back."

We couldn't understand what the problem was, although we had heard in passing that our admin was always on the phone with customers, so we knew she was working hard. Well, it's not enough to know that or to see someone working. It won't reveal a problem. What we found was a little ironic: calls were being missed because she was on the phone *so much*. We needed another phone line and a person who could answer it.

Customer service is a vital part of your company. When a customer calls, the first person they talk to is your administrator. If your phone isn't answered or they're not called back, what message does that send to your customer?

Often, when you grow fast, these points of contention appear, but they don't get the attention they need. They get overlooked because you're so busy putting out little fires and being reactive instead of proactive.

Until we called our phone provider, we had no idea that we could program our system to ring other areas in the office. Our receptionist was on the phone so much that when people called in, their calls went straight to voicemail. She would then send those voicemails off to the person the customer was looking for.

> **When communication comes to a person via voicemail, messages can get lost in transition.**

After we added a new person, we split the duties between the two admins and programed our phone system to ring to another line if both of them couldn't answer the phone within a few rings.

This is just one example of a simple fix that, when applied, made a huge difference in our company. But until we used outside eyeballs, we couldn't see it. We needed those eyeballs to help us do the work necessary to address the small details that make a huge difference to the customer.

We applied the same audit that resolved the admin department to fix other areas as well.

As a tax and accounting company, we can always anticipate a wave of customers flooding in right before business and personal tax deadlines. When they don't get their taxes filed on time, they point the finger back at us.

Sure, we could revert the blame to them and say, "Sorry, but you didn't get us your documentation in time. This isn't our fault." Which is true, in a sense, but not taking accountability for what we could do better or not finding a way to improve their experience doesn't help the situation or the client. After hearing these excuses from our clients, we had to create a role to fill that gap.

Now, three months before tax deadlines, we bring in interns. The interns' job is to call our customers months ahead of time, to help them prepare their organizers, to put them on the schedule to follow up with them, to procure their documents, and assist in building their organizers one by one.

With this new process, by the time tax deadlines come, we have most, if not all, of the documentation needed to file our customers on time. We've done as much as we can for the client. It's an expense to the company initially, but it's really more of an investment when we see the result of the time and issues solved.

In creating this new role, we've helped business owners get ahead of the game—which is what a lot of them need.

When we bring customers on board now, we tell them: "Our job is to help hold you accountable to get us what we need to service you to the best of our ability. So, we're going to annoy you sometimes. We're going to be persistent with you because it's for your benefit. We want to make sure that you get the service you need and deserve as a business owner. If you can't accept that we're going to be proactive with you, then this might not be the service for you. But if you know you need that kind of follow-up, that's what we are here for." We live by these words now.

The value of delegating your busy CEO work, of handing out the responsibilities you do in the trenches so you can spend time in other areas making improvements, is immeasurable. Tweaking what you might think are unimportant items is instrumental when it comes to the retention of your customers.

2. **Training**: Training was another area where we identified what processes needed to be addressed quickly. For so long, we hadn't had smooth training in our company. Every time we brought in a new employee to fill a new role, they trained under the current person in that role. Step by step, they'd walk the new employee through each spreadsheet and process as they divulged how they handled the role.

The problem with this approach was that it took time away from the leaders in our company. It shortchanged the key roles that produced the most revenue. For example, if your sales manager is also one of your highest producing representatives, but they can't spend time doing what they do best and making money for the company because they're training the new rep, you've got a problem. Ask yourself: *how much is it costing the company to keep that skilled key role away from closing sales to train a new person—who might not even work out in the company?*

It doesn't take a rocket scientist to see that our training strategy was backward, that we had created a very costly situation for the company and our employees. To magnify that issue, it was happening in every department.

Every time we hired a new accounting role or team lead, it happened. We spent more time training people in these new roles and pulling key people away from their positions. This even applied to our administrative roles—with a twist. Our admins were beyond busy in their roles. But when we hired a new admin to resolve their complications, it was almost like it had to get worse before it could get better. But it doesn't have to be that way. We just didn't address the problem soon enough. If you have the same concerns, you might not feel as much pain if you get after resolving them sooner.

The auditing company recommended that we outsource a company to help build and create our digital training modules so we could give back the time to our key players they were spending on training. We 100% agreed this needed to get done ASAP. So, we looked at several companies that specialized in doing this but, after pulling our team together, we felt it was worth incentivizing our best people to build the step-by-step training procedures for every process in that role. To get them even more excited about the prospect of doing this, we gave them bonuses for each instruction they put together.

It was something they could do in their downtime. Some employees were willing to give up their lunch breaks to work on this initiative, knowing they were making extra money.

It was a win-win situation that got the trainings done for each department. And we got that valuable time back, all while the team made extra income after hours.

Today, when we bring somebody into a new role, they spend their first week going through each training module. Instead of sitting right next to our more profitable people, they go through each training module. If they hit a bump in the road, they can ask the leader of that department, or their manager, what they would do in their position. Now, the new employee's questions are answered by the digital course. This allows our pivotal people to do what they do best, whether that's selling, fulfilling, or customer service.

> **The bottom line is investing in digital training for your business will be a huge tool in getting your departments running efficiently and effectively.**

When you can get new people up to speed in their roles quickly, these modules are your best friend in scaling your business to new levels.

3. **Structure Your Meetings:** We all know that having meetings is super important to your company, but they've got to be structured properly —or you are wasting your time.

When was the last time you attended a training to learn how to properly structure a meeting—so you and the other attendees would get the most out of it?

I can hear your reply, probably never. So many of us feel or have felt as though we have woken up in our roles. That the work we did initially in our companies transformed on us, and one day, we woke up in charge of a bunch of different items—meetings being one of them. When we launch our companies, we start out as a solo operator; then we get one employee and two and three, etc.

A team that size doesn't require a lot of meeting planning or structure. Unfortunately, as you grow and acquire more moving parts and departments, expanding to 50 employees, for instance, if you don't structure your meetings early, you'll just be winging it. You never want to wing it in any area of your business—especially where meetings, aka communication, are concerned. Meetings can be very powerful, or they can be quite counterproductive.

I know this very well because I've been through it.

As a small company, we had meetings with a handful of people. They were productive, and we only had them when we needed to. But as we grew, our meeting schedule stayed that way. Understand, once you get to a certain size, scheduling a meeting out of need doesn't work anymore.

We assessed what we were doing with the auditing company, and they identified that we needed to have more structured meetings.

Our Monday morning meetings with our sales department were held to motivate the team. We always want more sales, which means more revenue, leading to more pay. Having these meetings helped to facilitate that. We knew we could make a massive impact on the bottom line by creating structured meetings in all departments of the company. Well-structured meetings are mandatory to make sure you have a well-oiled machine.

Using meetings to boost growth is possible, but you can also misuse meetings resulting in a death-by-meeting situation. This is when you have too many unproductive meetings.

We didn't want any of our meetings to suffer.

An example of an unproductive meeting would be trying your damnedest to solve problems but encountering too many people giving their input. Then before you know it, people are out of control and going off on tangents.

Maybe originally, you had called the meeting to solve a certain problem but ended the meeting talking about five other topics. When people and agendas get out of control, there's no clear direction of who's going to solve what and how to identify the deadlines. In this case, all you did was get in there and talk about the problem. You didn't create a solution—and that's a big problem.

We found ourselves in this tight spot. A further complication was that nobody was leading the meetings. Our leadership team had no clear direction or deadlines to solve problems.

Through the audit process, we learned we were only holding weekly meetings with certain departments and when there were problems to solve.

That's backward.

The idea is to cut problems off at the pass—*before* they are problems. Since that audit, we have now structured quarterly meetings with partners, and we have monthly meetings with our leaders.

Our leaders, in turn, have weekly meetings with their departments to start the week—including the long-standing sales meetings.

Our meetings are much more structured now. When we have quarterly meetings, someone leads the meeting with the partners. And since we have a clearer overview of our company, we can identify minor tweaks before they spiral. Our monthly meetings delegate any issues that are still manageable to our leaders.

At that point, our leaders can identify the people on their teams who are the best resources to solve their problems. They can assign a deadline for it to be solved. Then they can follow up with these appointed problem solvers in their weekly meetings. There, they can make sure tasks are on schedule to be solved; if they're not, they can pivot the plan to get that person the help they need to stick to the deadline.

Structuring your meetings will make a noticeable difference in your company. Every company will be different, but when you go into each properly led meeting, you'll spend less time in the meeting room. Structured meetings are also more productive and less prone to tangents which is what makes meetings unproductive and drag out longer than they need, depriving time needed to address duties.

I highly recommend that you figure out how you can structure your meetings. Your plan should be based on the size of your company. If you follow our plan, you'll set quarterly meetings, then make sure that you always show up. If someone can't make one of your meetings, don't cancel them. You have an agenda for that meeting, so it will be productive and valuable to you. Stick to it no matter what—even if some of your attendees can't make it.

Too many businesses that we see and work with make one of two mistakes. 1) They don't have enough meetings or 2) they have too many meetings.

Run your meetings as I just described in this point, and you will thank me a year from now.

Quick Tip: Make some meetings fun. We do an annual retreat with our key leaders. On these retreats, we plan out our next year, then break to have fun together on the golf course, mountain biking slopes, while kayaking, boating, etc. These offsite locations are wonderful for further bonding the team.

Effective Team-Building Takeaways

Until you have a good base of systems, processes, and checklists in place, you won't be the most effective networker.

To scale and grow, you need to be out cultivating valuable relationships that bring in more sales, but if you bring in more revenue and work without the right systems in place to scale, you'll just scale a mess that will eventually implode.

You can't do it all alone. Your employees, key players, and partners, are a part of your valuable network. It's a great strategy to believe in them and let them know it by trusting them to step up and take more off your plate. Then you can focus even more on the relationship capital of your business.

Before you move on to the next chapter, ask yourself: Are you willing to let go of control in your roles to allow your team to step up and take over? (They will make mistakes and go through some learning curves, but they will also surprise you at times with how they can eventually perform better than you.)

Are you willing to do the extra work to formulate the systems that will lead to the rewards of more freedom, better results for your teams, and better results for your customer?

Are you willing to take strategic steps back? Sometimes, you need to take two steps back to fine-tune details and enable a giant leap forward. Sometimes, you must dig in deeper, work more hours, and spend more dollars for a short period of time, so you can gain back precious time freedom.

CHAPTER 15

MAGNETIC MOVES

"If you want to be seen, you have to put yourself out there. It's that simple!"
—Karen Fossum

As I've made clear throughout this book, you must be a person people are drawn to so you can be an ultimate networker.

That means getting strategic and tactical about attracting the right attention from the right people.

Now, it's time to execute some magnetic moves to get those desired relationships seeking you out as well!

I put together five magnetic strategies that will absolutely get you the attention you want. Unfortunately, executing the steps is not easy for most people.

People, in general, are extremely scared of rejection and fear. So much so that they allow what others think about them to paralyze them from any willingness to put themselves out there and make these magnetic moves. (Don't do that! Push through it, and you will see it gets so much easier.)

**We can all see the pattern of success.
It's in those who are willing to do what others won't. They are the ones living the lives that most want but don't have.**

To get to this place, do what you have to do to become magnetic. Start pushing yourself to do more of what others are scared to do. Sure, you will suck for a while but failing forward for a period of time until you get good is exactly how you're going to get what you want.

Six Magnetic Moves to Attract Valuable People to Your Network

1. **Events and Groups**: A great place to meet new people who are successful in the niches where you are trying to grow is at events and in groups. You can try your local BNI (Business Network International) groups. I was part of one called Corporate Alliance, for instance. Also, check out your local Chamber of Commerce and small business expos. Wherever you call home, there are groups and meetups that can put you in touch with thousands of people who have the same goal you do—camaraderie and finding resources. I joined these organizations to shake hands and meet new people. While that always does lead to expanding your circle, you still want to be a part of higher-level events and groups.

    Even in the early days of launching your business, make it a part of your strategy to get into those higher-end groups. Some of them even cost six figures a year to be a part of—but they are worth it, and that investment with people who don't play when it comes to business always pays off—and more than you put in.

    I then worked my way up to get my own booths at some of the larger events to try and attract more people to me. No matter what you're doing, make sure you're drawing a lot of people to you. Remember, above anything else, to be strategic. Understand who's leading the events and/or groups, and make sure they're people that you want to do business with.

    Once I know who's in charge, I pull what I call a magnetic move, meaning I sponsor their events. Paying for your sponsorship is a smart way to get some one-on-one time with people who have next-level influence in your niche or industry. This allows you to develop a relationship with them. Yes, doing this is costly, so let's revert to earlier in the book when we talked about how important it is to get your money right early on.

Paying for those extra eyeballs as a sponsor is a way to leverage the money you've set aside in your business to enable opportunities like these. I cultivated the relationship with one of my most valuable and current groups by getting my foot in the door by investing $10,000 to sponsor their event. That turned into multiple phone conversations with the person who I knew I wanted to do business with (since I had done my research), and it led to many other valuable relationships. That's an investment that makes sense.

be afraid to go to these events. Don't be afraid to spend a little money to get into them. These big events are great places to start practicing shaking hands and getting to know people. This is where you will hone the skill of becoming approachable. Just make sure that you don't carry yourself like a jerk.

To share a quick story with you on how I actually capitalized on somebody else being a jerk, I was at a pretty high-level event with multi-6-figure and 7-figure business operators. I joined in on the conversation of a small group of people since I wanted to connect with a person in that group.

As the conversation went on, I heard a gentleman tell one of the other fellows that he was pretty proud of himself because, for the first time, he had broken through a quarter-million dollars in personal revenue. The other person laughed and said, "That's funny, man. I paid that much in taxes this year."

> **Instantly his comment diminished the guy who was so proud of his new level. Lesson learned: don't boast at the expense of other people. But don't boast anyway. It's gross.**

After that jerk's comment, people scattered. I approached the scorned man and said, "Dude, I think it's awesome that you broke a new personal record and took home a quarter-million dollars. I can tell there's much more to come for you."

Shortly after that, I learned that he is in a niche that aligns with my business! He was an ideal referral partner for me. Now keep in mind, I'm an accounting business owner for small business owners, and this guy is a web developer helping other small business owners get their websites off the ground or rebuilt. That's a perfect target audience for me to sell my startup accounting packages to.

We created a referral partner relationship. Since then, I've done over $400,000 in sales in my first year doing business with this gentleman. So, while it's a sound strategy for you to attend these events and join these groups, it's also a wise idea to map out a plan before you attend and find out who else is a part of these events and groups.

Nowadays, on social media, you can see who's attending these events. Do a little research on their personal social pages and find out who aligns with your business, who could be your ideal client or referral partner, or who could help to enhance your business.

Being an authentic and genuine person in the way you carry yourself at these events will magnetize more people to you.

How you draw people to you comes down to confidence. Everyone is attracted to confidence. If you possess real confidence in yourself, you won't need to tear others down to try and lift yourself up.

2. **Social Media Magnet:** Social media is a key area you must focus on to get other people's attention. It can be overwhelming trying to figure out the best strategies to apply on social media, so let me share what I've done that's been super powerful in attracting people.

First, as I mentioned, you need to become strategic. Your first step is to identify all the people you want to do business with and who you want to align with. Then you need to follow those people and pay close attention to them.

Typically, people of influence aren't going to comment back and respond to your direct messages. They're busy running businesses. You're not going to grab their attention until you start taking attention-grabbing action.

First, it's a great idea to start sharing their content and tagging them in the content that you share. In this way, you'll let them know that you appreciate them. But keep this in mind before you rush off and start writing posts; you need to be consistent in doing this once you start.

Getting connected to one of my current mentors took four years of taking consistent actions. As I've worked toward becoming more aligned with them, I've developed a friendship with them, and we do business together, as well as this person also refers me business. It took two years to get to the point of doing business with him. It took four years to develop the friendship that we now have.

This type of payoff doesn't happen overnight, but again, it is worth it.

For this tactic to work, you will have to do a few things that are uncomfortable. First, you'll have to start posting often—as in every single day. You won't just share your influencer's content; you'll post your own. So get comfortable writing, putting your feelings out there on multiple social media platforms, and sharing your knowledge.

When you do this, in addition to creating content that will get you noticed, you will also be giving back to your communities. Everybody has something to learn from everybody. The best thing you can do as you are learning about your business and life is share it and put it out there. The right people will read it; the right people will resonate with it, and the right people will message you.

As you are posting, share your wins. Yes, it might put a spotlight on you that you're not used to, and it will attract some hate and negativity, but it will attract far more positivity and curiosity from people who want to win, too. That's who you want to connect with anyway. It's essential that you know your social platforms are a form of your ecosystem. It's important to protect what you're exposed to. So, clean them up and arrange them so you can see what you want and hide what you don't. These platforms are all programmed to show you more of what you're interested in, so spend some time consuming positive, productive content. You will get more of that back.

Make sure you follow more people who put out good content and vibes that you align with. As you do this, clean out the people who you know would love to see you fail.

Trust me; people are always watching you. Some of the people with who you could never dream of doing business are usually not as far away or as hard to connect with as you think. But they need to see your content and that you align with them before they make the move to get to know you.

3. **Power of Writing**: I never thought that writing would be such a big part of my life, yet here I am in the middle of creating this book. I also didn't think I would enjoy it—even though I felt the pull to put it out on the market. For a long time, I didn't even like reading books.

> **But here's the deal. Writing works.
> Writing in various places to bring
> influence your way works, too.**

I was lucky enough to have a mentor who showed me the value of writing. As a part of Ryan Stewman's mastermind, he encouraged his group to write a book. He also encouraged us to write articles and put ourselves out there, to start putting in the writing repetition that leads to becoming great writers. The people who want to grow and the right types of people you want to bring into your network are people who will read the kinds of articles you write.

Writing is just one more way for you to be out in the world. It's also evergreen. People will find what you have written for years and even generations to come.

You earn clout and validity when your articles are published in places like *Forbes*, *Business.com*, or other places that set the pace in multiple industries and have established themselves as a credible resource in the marketplace.

When you see writing opportunities on major media sites, seize them. It only takes one or two mentions in an article before you can use them to your advantage.

Getting placed in top-tier sites should be a part of your long-term strategy. Not only will it give you creditability, but it will start getting you attention from people with more influence. So, make sure you share those wins on your social media as your writing gets featured in bigger publications. This is a great way to leverage bigger opportunities.

People with influence want to align with other people of influence. It's a reciprocal value, so you need to offer that same level of value.

If you're not a great writer, that's okay. Hire an editor, a writing coach, or a vetted PR firm to get you started. That's what I did! It has led to more friends and more opportunities like speaking engagements. When you're introduced at an event as being featured in *Forbes* or as a published author, you grab much more attention from the audience, and your message becomes more powerful.

4. **Say Yes to Speaking on Stages**: I always wanted to speak on stage. When I was a sales guy working for several different companies and met speakers from those companies, I admired them. They seemed to operate at a different level.

When I got the opportunity to speak at an event for the first time, I instantly said yes. But right after I did, I also instantly felt doubt and insecurity. I understand why people say that speaking is one of their biggest fears.

My first opportunity to speak was tough! During the gig, the slides I'd prepared didn't work. Then I suffered terrible cotton-mouth, and I hadn't brought any water up on stage with me. My hands got sweaty. My heart pounded out of my chest, and I got completely off course.

When I walked off stage, I thought I had failed. Then the event broke for lunch, and I was swarmed by a group of individuals wanting information about our company. When I talked to them one by one, they told me all about their problems with their taxes and accounting. They actually wanted to talk more with me about how they could solve their problems. As I stood there among these hungry people, I instantly knew the value of speaking.

The second you step onto a stage, people admire you for your willingness to get up there—because most won't. An old true saying by Les

Brown is: "You must be willing to do the things today others won't do, in order to have the things tomorrow others won't have."

I've simplified it a bit: "To get what others don't have, you have to be willing to do what others won't." Speaking is one of those things.

Anytime you have an opportunity to speak, say yes.

Most likely, you'll suck at first. But as you do more, you'll get better—something I'm still practicing myself. After speaking a dozen times and getting better, my influence is growing. More influence will bring you more connections. More connections will bring you more clients.

My rule of thumb is when speaking opportunities come your way, say yes, then figure it out. The more prepared you are, the more impactful you'll be. I made a crucial mistake my first time speaking when I thought I knew what I was talking about—that I could just wing it. I half-assed prepared instead of making sure I was extra prepared.

Once you say yes, get to work and practice, then prepare to give the best speech of your life.

5. **Start a Podcast**: One of the best things I ever did for my business and network was start a podcast with my partner, Trevor. We wouldn't have launched our podcast if not for the groups we were a part of. That's why joining groups is the number one to-do in this chapter. The bonus is that it led to us hosting our podcast.

At the time we talked about launching our podcast, we had already written scripts and content to make us a little more visible on social media. Although we had signed up to do speaking gigs and had cranked out a few videos, it was starting the podcast that was so powerful.

We didn't know what we were doing when we were trying to get the podcast off the ground, but I remember, after leaving a couple of events in St. Louis, Missouri, saying to Trevor, "People who are at the level we want to be at have a podcast. We should start one, too." We both knew it was going to take time and be a big commitment, but we also understood that having our own show would get us closer to the influencers we wanted to do business with. I told him: "If we can get these guys on our podcast and we can get on their podcasts, it'll be a win-win for us."

Trevor and I made a commitment that as soon as we got home, we would order the podcast equipment.

For the first show, we did an introductory episode to introduce who we were and our backgrounds. Then we made the commitment to consistently put out episodes for the next three to five years to determine what type of success the podcast would create for us. We knew going into it that it was going to take a long time to gain traction, but we were up for it.

My friend, an owner of an agency that helps people launch podcasts, told me that most influencers won't entertain being on a podcast until they see that the host has recorded at least 20 episodes. That's because most failed podcasts die around the fifteenth episode when the host pulls the plug because they haven't seen the results they want.

Today, we are glad we started our podcast, *Real Business Owners*. After two and a half years, it ranks in the top 1% of business podcasts and has brought us an incredible number of clients. The best part is that it has given us a long list of guests who want to be on our podcast—and they are also people we want to do business with.

When you stay consistent and eventually establish a platform, people who want to grow their platform will naturally want to be a part of a podcast where they can leverage some of your viewership.

While getting used to speaking on camera and through a podcast might feel unnatural, just like the name of this book implies, you need to be willing to do what is uncomfortable.

If you worry about what to talk about, don't forget that content is all around you. You can always come up with subjects to speak on. What you speak on will attract people who will be your listeners. Loyal listeners will get to know you, like you, and trust you based on your show that they tune in to every single week. The sooner you get started, the quicker you'll see the success.

It's also a great idea to record your podcasts in video form because we've learned it's quite effective in growing your social media audience. We simply take our hottest episode moments, chop them up into shorty clips and run them as paid promotions. Even a twenty-dollar boost can get thousands of more eyeballs on your show.

When you have all the eyeballs watching you and start creating your own influence, guess what happens? People with influence will ask to be on your show.

6. **Create Your Own Groups**: Creating your own groups, events, networking groups, and masterminds is an ultimate magnet move. Currently, we've created smaller-scale groups, but we've also been a part of a lot of very high-level groups with business-minded people.

   The amount of power in these groups is hard to explain. We've paid close attention to how much the level of influence has grown from the founders of each one of these groups. From the smaller-scale groups to the super high-level groups, the people who create the groups always have the most influence.

That's because people always seek to belong. If you can create a group where people feel a sense of belonging, they will want to be as close to the leader of that community as possible. Community leaders have that next level of influence because of the risks they've taken to put themselves out there and form these groups. Every member must go through the founder to be a part of these groups.

As you get to know the people in the communities you create, you can learn a lot about what people are there for.

As long as you pay close attention to who your people are and their needs, you'll have the opportunity to connect members with the right people, too. When that happens, and you become a connector of the right people within your community, good things will happen. In making an impact on people's lives like that, not only are they going to be more loyal to you, but they'll want to bring more people to you.

After you see significant results from speaking, investing with others, putting your content out there on social media, writing, and making your videos, make sure that you are paying close attention to all the things that work and don't work on your journey. Once you get to that point, it's time to create your own group. Use your skillsets to help people who trust you and buy into your culture to help them. When you do, your influence will only grow.

Once you've built up a certain amount of influence in your groups, you will attract people with their own groups, who will want to speak to your crowd and share your audience with their audience. This is a ladder for many people that leads to new levels as well as links you with their influencers.

Putting It All Together

These recommendations are a combination of old and new-school networking. They are more successful when you use them together. Some of the old-school ways like going to events, throwing your own affair, writing a book, creating your own brand, and courses are all potent ways to prove yourself as an authority in the marketplace. These tactics still work because people want to be a part of a community they're attracted to.

I've always gravitated toward the entrepreneurship community. I've gone to their events, put on some of our own similar to theirs, and have participated in activities like writing a book. When you undertake these activities, it attracts more people to you who also want to be a part of that community.

The new way of doing business marketing entails social media and networking. Nowadays, we can throw events and meet virtually on Zoom. These applications make the world a bit smaller. More people can attend and be a part of your community—we are much more accessible. The social media aspect alone is a significant way to attract more people to you.

However you're conducting yourself, it doesn't make it any easier to put yourself out there. Being criticized is still one of our strongest fears. The only way through it is to practice using your voice and letting people see your face.

Tapping into your willingness will be an advantageous tool for you. Make videos. Put them out there on your social media channels. Boost your posts. Throw a little ad spin behind them. Be willing to take on constructive criticism. Learn, and adapt, but continue to be you because eventually, the right people will stay.

As you improve and become more influential, you'll want to put on your own events. You'll want to speak more. You'll even want to do more videos. It might seem hard to believe now, but that is the truth.

Be willing to give and receive. As you do so, it will empower you to keep giving, to become more influential, to make more of an impact in other people's lives. No matter what type of business you're in, tapping into the power of networking will attract more of the right people to you.

Get the network coming to you!

Get the business coming to you!

Get strategic on where you're spending your time and in the content you put out across all platforms.

BE WILLING to get started and put yourself out there.

Start implementing these strategies and watch what happens over the next two years. It will forever change your trajectory, and your network will continue leveling up!

Chapter 16

STRONG LEADERSHIP CREATES YOUR BULLETPROOF REPUTATION

"Self-leadership is about awareness, tolerance and not letting your own natural tendencies limit your potential."
—Scott Belsky

Throughout this book, we've talked a lot about tactics you can take to make yourself more attractive in the marketplace. We've talked about what you can use to become a magnet to opportunity—a person others will seek out to do business with.

In this last chapter, I'm going to help you understand how and why it's so important to become a better leader.

Leadership is a never-ending journey. When you are a leader, there is always more to learn and more to practice to continue evolving.

It's up to you to know where you need to improve so you can continue leading yourself and others. By leading and creating movements, groups, or opportunities that people want to be a part of, you can become the ultimate networker. Understand, leadership is the ultimate power move in being an ultimate networker.

As you're developing into a leader seeking to gain the trust of other people, there are a few phases to be conscious of. Let's go through them.

Leadership Phases

1. **Become a Leader of Yourself:** Before you can be a leader, you have to become a leader of yourself and your actions.

   Even though I explained my history in great detail, what I needed may not be the same as what you need.

   What I taught you in this book, for example, the A. B. C. D. E. method, may not be what you want to do or what will work for you. It definitely worked for me because it made me practice what I needed daily for years. I stayed committed to practicing it long-term and developed the discipline, self-awareness, and confidence to lead others. But to even embark on that journey, I had to start by leading and being honest with myself. I had to finally take action on those methods I practiced.

   Doing so required a great deal of faith in the outcome that I couldn't see. I didn't know if I was going to become a better man. I didn't know if I was going to become a great leader by doing worksheets and continuing to practice year after year. I just had to commit with faith and do the work.

   In becoming diligent in the A. B. C. D. E. method and fine-tuning the "what" versus "why" questions, I developed a higher self-awareness. This is important to know because self-awareness is going to be the key for you to become a great leader and an ultimate networker.

   Had I not gone through all those years of being a leader of myself and developing self-awareness, I would've never been aware of my anger. I would've never been aware of the pre-judgment that I was constantly practicing. I wouldn't have been fully aware of when I was operating out of greed.

Commit to being a self-directed leader. Get structured and get the gains you need to become a great leader of others.

2. **Be a Great Follower:** No matter what level you're at, you need leaders. You must seek out other leaders to continue growing as a leader. So while you may become a great leader, you will always need to understand that you will be a follower—as long as you are on a leadership journey yourself.

3. **Maintain Humility:** Willingness and humility go hand in hand. You can't have one without the other.

If you want to have humility, you must be willing to be in that position. If you want to tap into the power of willingness, you must have enough humility to realize that you don't always have it figured out. You must be willing to take on the journey of becoming a person of humility.

Humility is the art of acceptance.

Accept that you don't have it all figured out.

Accept that you need help.

Accept being open.

Do not close off other opinions, options, or constructive criticism. Be open to other ideas or paths. There are no great leaders without humility.

Great leaders realize there's always work to be done. If they say they're going to do something, they know they must follow through and do it.

When you do the work required, seek out other great leaders, and tap into the willingness to maintain being a person of humility, you will have the greatest asset on your side as a networker, operator, and business person. This builds a strong reputation.

I've seen the most growth in my business from having a strong and well-maintained reputation. My first 15 years in business were built from relationships and referral partners. I felt rewarded when people called me because of my reputation. After putting in the time I needed to, I was finally known as someone who was easy to work with, who always paid on time, who did what I said I was going to do, who made things right if I needed to, and who always went out of my way to make connections and/or efforts to improve my business and network, as well.

Other people speaking highly of you and vouching for you is still the most powerful form of closing.

I recently attended a mastermind in 2021 with 100 men and women who are higher-level business operators. There were many 8-figure and 9-figure business owners present. During those three days, we had a little breakout session and separated into smaller groups. As you can imagine, with over 100 people in attendance, there's something special about these breakout sessions when you break down into 10 different groups of just 10 people.

Each breakout session was headed by one of the more influential members of the mastermind. On this day, I was in attendance at Ryan Stewman's breakout session. Alongside him was another friend of mine, Kurt Linington. We went around the table, introduced ourselves, talked about what our needs were, what we were looking to get out of the mastermind, and if there was anything people could help with. This is a powerful exercise within many masterminds. The main

STRONG LEADERSHIP CREATES YOUR BULLETPROOF REPUTATION

premise of this mastermind was investments. Most of the attendees were business owners at the investor level of their business. Their businesses were running themselves, so everybody was seeking out additional ways to get their money working for them.

Kurt, who runs a 9-figure business, talked to the group and helped another gentleman solve his problem before he left to use the restroom. As he was walking off, Ryan Stewman, another high-level entrepreneur, said, "That guy right there is no joke. He doesn't jump into any investment without dotting his I's and crossing his Ts, without doing all the research required to know if it's a solid investment. Everything he touches turns to gold."

It's funny when people say things like, "Everything he touches turns to gold." Those sorts of results don't come without an extreme amount of hard work, without failures, overcoming those failures, self-leadership, and strong leadership of others. When you are a person with strong leadership over yourself and other people, you develop a reputation, and in turn, people of influence like Ryan Stewman will make remarks like that behind your back.

Naturally, when Kurt came back to the table, everybody wanted more insight from him. They wanted his phone number and to do deals with him. We were all curious about what Kurt was investing in, including me.

You have to realize there are levels to investing. I've been the person who other people talk about when they say, "Man, everything he touches turns to gold." But to be that person at such a high level when other 8-figure and 9-figure business owners are present is powerful. Kurt is now known by people who have exited their businesses for over a billion dollars. They are saying, "That's the guy you want to do deals with."

That's powerful.

Everybody should strive for that level of reputation.

When you focus on what we've talked about throughout this entire book, you can be in that position, too.

Start by reprogramming the story you were told in your upbringing—the one that is so limiting to you. Reprogram yourself to be the person you want to become. Live the type of life you want to live by doing the work required and being your own strong leader. That's the only way to rise to the next phase of becoming a great leader of other people.

When you are a great leader of other people, maintain humility. When you stay humble enough to do the work always required and follow through with what you say you're going to do, you create and earn a strong reputation.

On the flip side, if you're a person who will not tap into the willingness to change your environments, to double down and practice developing the skill sets that you need to thrive in your business, the opposite happens.

Somebody vouching for you is one of the most powerful tools you can use to attract more people to you. When you are this kind of person, people want to do business with you. But if nobody can vouch for you, you will learn that people will say quite the opposite. They will talk about how you don't follow through and don't do what's required. They will highlight your failures instead of your successes. In that case, people won't need to pre-judge you because others will have already judged you by the experiences you've created for them. When people talk about you like that, it does the opposite of magnetizing people to you; it pushes them away.

STRONG LEADERSHIP CREATES YOUR BULLETPROOF REPUTATION

I hope you have found a great deal of value in each chapter and can understand why it's so important to start leading yourself and develop the reputation required to continue growing.

Remember, wealth is more than a measurement of the amount of money you have. While money is powerful and can be a potent tool for you in continuing to grow and impact your life and others' lives, wealth means nothing without a wealth of happiness.

Your network will determine how far you go and how happy you are.

I commend you for finishing what you started and encourage you to keep going. Results are always on the other side of seeing your intentions through.

We've covered many leadership attributes in this book, and while all can give you a certain edge, every single one of them starts with willingness.

Ask yourself, *what am I willing to face today to become a person of accountability? What can I mentally, physically, and emotionally address right now to become a better leader and attract the right people to me?*

Formulate your answers and plan.

Then do it.

ACKNOWLEDGMENTS

I can't even picture my life without all the amazing experiences brought by my awesome network of people, so let me thank a few of them in my life.

My incredible wife and children are the reason I push through to continue building an amazing life.

My amazing business partners have brought so much support and experience to our journey in business. I have learned so much from them.

My mentors starting with Steve, my therapist, and all the powerful masterminds and creators of those mastermind groups that I have been fortunate to be a part of. Apex, Arete, Avengers Master Mind, and The Insider investors, I can only hope you all continue on forever to make an impact on others' lives like you have on mine.

My network of referral partners and clients over the years for how much they have taught me through the years. How I wish I would have read a book about networking versus figuring it all out for myself so I could have served you greater sooner.

And lastly ...

The people who helped me through the creation of this book. Hilary and her team for guiding me with their expertise and helping me make this a readable and enjoyable experience for the people who need it.

I am beyond grateful for everyone who played a role in this first book of mine.

Thank you!

About The Author

Kale Goodman is a family man and entrepreneur. His two main passions are leading his family and helping entrepreneurs build amazing lives.

It wasn't always that way. Kale grew up in a home of financial ruin and limited beliefs. Even though he always wanted success, he found failure. When he was younger, he lacked seeing his goals through and finishing anything. HELL! He didn't even finish high school!

After several failed businesses, partnerships, and relationships, he was pushed into personal growth and reprogramming who he is. Although he was unwilling at first to change his circumstances, he felt he had no choice but to pivot after losing it all. That's when everything changed!

Since then, he has lived a 5-year journey of consistent growth and has not only built an amazing family of his own but has become a 7-figure investor, scaled multiple 7-figure business ventures, and grown his main business EASIER ACCOUNTING to become an 8-figure accounting firm.

His secret to success involves mastering the art of leveraging relationships, attracting the right people to him, and helping underdog entrepreneurs realize their own missions.

To learn more about becoming an Ultimate Marketing Machine, visit KaleGoodman.com.

DISCLAIMER

Kale Goodman is not a licensed therapist or licensed financial professional.

Although he owns multiple businesses in the financial space and has many great experiences, which he shares throughout this book, and they have proven to be highly successful lessons for him, he always recommends that people seek advice from professionals of their choosing for more customized advice to their needs before implementing any strategies for themselves.

This content is not to be construed as advice but rather is the retelling of the author's life events for entertainment purposes only. Neither Kale nor his publisher is responsible for any results you may experience from implementing any of the content in this book in any capacity.

Made in the USA
Middletown, DE
28 January 2024